Downsizing Your Home
WITH STYLE

LIVING WELL IN A SMALLER SPACE

Lauri Ward

Downsizing Your Home
WITH STYLE

Collins

An Imprint of HarperCollinsPublishers

Photographs

All photographs by Lauri Ward except photo p. 90 by Tracy Taylor Ward.

Room Refinement™

All rooms refined by Lauri Ward except: pp. xxiii (bottom right), 4, 14, 15, 16, 18, 64, 147 (bottom right), 155 (top left), rooms refined by Rita Grossman; pp. 60, 90, 106, rooms refined by Tracy Taylor Ward.

Trademarks of Lauri Ward

Use What You Have®	Resale-Ready™
Interior Refiners Network®	Room Refinement™
Interior Refiner™	Color Refinement™
Interior Refinement™	Art & Accessory Refinement™

HarperCollins books may be purchased for educational, business, or sales promotional use. For information, please write: Special Markets Department, HarperCollins Publishers, 10 East 53rd Street, New York, NY 10022.

FIRST EDITION

Designed by Cassandra J. Pappas

Library of Congress Cataloging-in-Publication Data
Ward, Lauri.
  Downsizing your home with style : living well in a smaller space / Lauri Ward.—1st ed.
    p. cm.
  Includes index.
  ISBN 978-0-06-117097-3
  1. House cleaning. 2. Moving, Household. 3. Orderliness. 4. Simplicity. I. Title.
  TX324.W35 2007
  648'.5—dc22

2007025235

06 07 08 09 10 ID/TP 10 9 8 7 6 5 4 3 2 1

To my aunts, uncles, and cousins,

who were so good to me when I was a little girl:

Frances, Herman, Arlene, and Linda Devins

Gus, Irene, Nadine, and Richard Rovin

Jack, Lucille, Leslie, and Alene Rovin

Alexander, Amalia, Elizabeth, Morris,

and Michael Salomon

And, especially, my wonderful grandmother Lillian

and my dearest uncles Steven and Herbert

Acknowledgments

Many thanks to the following people for their support:

To Joe Ward, who produces the photos for my books and who, for me, makes everything possible. I am lucky to have so talented a husband as my business partner.

To Liv Blumer, who believed in this project from the outset and who championed it every step of the way. Book after book, I continue to be grateful to her for all of her guidance over the past decade.

To Mary Ellen O'Neill at Collins, whose vision for this book was spot on from the beginning. It has been a pleasure collaborating with her after hearing about her for so many years.

To all of the loyal *Use What You Have* clients, and especially those whose homes appear in this book: It is because of them that all of this is possible.

To Judy Kern, who has been such a great help over the years and who has taught me so much. One day I am going to get my hands on her house!

To Tracy Taylor Ward, who continues to make me proud. I am thankful for having such a wonderful daughter who not only has become my colleague at *Use What You Have* but who is also working as a decorator/host on HGTV.

To Rita Grossman, who was the first decorator trained in the *Use What You Have* system and who has been my faithful friend and favorite junking buddy for decades.

To the *Use What You Have* decorators and staff, who keep our clients happy and our business running smoothly. All of their fine work is deeply appreciated.

To the members of the Interior Refiners Network,® who are a constant source of inspiration and who are carrying the torch by making their clients' homes and lives more beautiful and comfortable. I am honored to have trained them.

To the talented people at HarperCollins whose efforts produced this book and to whom I am grateful: Laura Dozier, editorial assistant; Jean Marie Kelly, marketing manager; Felicia Sullivan, online marketing manager; Amy Vreeland, production editor; Georgia Morrissey, art director; Cassandra Pappas, book designer; Shelby Meizlik, senior director of publicity; April Ferreira, publicist.

And, finally, to my family and friends who mean so much to me. I am grateful for their love.

I had three chairs in my house: one for solitude, two for friendship, three for society.

—*Henry David Thoreau, the ultimate downsizer*

Contents

Introduction:
Living More Simply
Is the Best Revenge

There are many reasons why you might be moving to a smaller home. Maybe your children have left the nest and you're ready to fly the coop to a smaller, more manageable home, or maybe you're about to return to the city after living in the suburbs for a couple of decades. Perhaps you're exchanging one large home for two smaller ones—summer and winter or a suburban condo and a city pied-à-terre. Maybe you're following the southern and southwestern migration. You might be relocating to accept your dream job or retiring and trying to reallocate your disposable income. Perhaps you just want to simplify your life so that there's "less work for Mother." Or you could be downsizing for quite a few other reasons.

Whatever your motivation, moving is always stressful, but downsizing is more about adapting than it is about moving. When you're telescoping a lifetime's accumulation of belongings from a larger home into a jewel box, the task can seem overwhelming, and so can your emotions. How do you decide what to pack and what to part with? Where will you put the contents of your attic, basement, and garage?

What if the ceilings are lower—or in some cases higher—the windows are smaller, and the living room rug would fill the entire space? How can you use the stuff you've got so that it functions well and looks right?

Perhaps you've spent your adult life up to this point moving to larger and larger homes. If so, reversing that pattern will be a dramatic change. But I urge you not to look upon it as a compromise. Rather, I want you to embrace it, approach the change positively, and think about what you'll be gaining, not losing. When you reduce what you have to the best and most loved, your new space will be even more special, and just because you have less space doesn't mean that it can't be even more stylish. In fact, you may actually be upgrading some of your furnishings, your appliances, or other accoutrements.

That said, the emotional component of "letting go" may be more difficult for some than for others. Those of you who clean out your closets regularly and tend to throw things away instead of hanging on to them "just in case" will have an easier time than those who still have a black-and-white television stashed in the attic and the stub from every bill they've ever paid. Downsizing is as much about making an emotional commitment to change as it is about figuring out where to put your furniture. It's about living more simply and calmly, making that choice in advance and living it in the future. It's about leading a richer life by having less.

My goal for this book is to provide you with all the strategies you'll need to alleviate your anxiety, overcome emotional barriers, and make sure your new home is as lovely, livable, and low maintenance as possible.

From the moment you find your new space until you've been living in it for a year, I will guide you step-by-step through the mental and physical processes that can make your move cathartic and creative instead of catastrophic. You may not have downsized before, but I've helped clients do it hundreds, if not thousands, of times. In fact, as a

New York City–based Interior Refiner™ for thirty years, I like to think of myself as an expert on helping space-challenged clients solve their dilemmas. And now many of my New York clients are downsizing to smaller homes in various states, including Florida (where Use What You Have® also has an office), Arizona, New Mexico, Colorado, and other locations that are closer to their previous homes. Since I have the experience and expertise to anticipate and avoid problems you may not be aware of, you'll be benefiting from my accumulated bag of tricks for decorating sleight of hand, camouflage, and storage. You'll be using what you have, and what I know, to take you from an empty space to a well-furnished nest, albeit a smaller one, without too many ruffled feathers.

The Ten Most Common Decorating Mistakes You Don't Have to Make

In my previous books I described the ten mistakes most people make when decorating their homes. I generally see them immediately when I arrive for a consultation, but most people don't recognize that these easy-to-solve problems are preventing them from feeling completely happy and comfortable in their living space.

You, however, are lucky! Rectifying these problems is even more important when you have space constraints. But you're moving, so, being forewarned, you can avoid making them in the first place. I'll describe each of them here, and once you're aware of them, you'll find them referred to again and again in the chapters that follow.

1. Not defining your priorities.

If you don't sort out what you have and make a plan in advance, you may find yourself moving into a crammed, cramped space and spending money to move things you don't want or can't use.

Whether you're buying or renting and how long you plan to stay will influence how much money you choose to spend on structural

To create a comfortable conversation area, the coffee table should always be within easy reach of the sofa.

changes as well as whether you paint or wallpaper, and even what colors you paint.

Think about how you'll be spending your time in your new home. If you expect to have frequent overnight guests, or plan to entertain often, that will affect how you design your downsized living space. So think about as many of these lifestyle factors as you can, and plan for them in advance.

2. Creating an uncomfortable conversation area.

This is one of the biggest and most frequent mistakes I find when I visit clients' homes, and I'll be talking a lot about how you can avoid it in the pages that follow. Basically, a comfortable conversation area is one in which all participants can talk to one another without raising their voices and twisting in their seats, and where they can all reach a table on which to set a plate or a glass without stretching uncomfortably or getting up from their seat.

Doing this the right way is particularly important when space is at a premium. If it is done wrong, you may arrange seating in a place where it won't be used, which means you'll be wasting space, or you may be obstructing people's ability to walk comfortably through the room.

In Chapter 2 I'll be describing the five best ways to configure a comfortable, U-shaped conversation area and how you can use the pieces you already have to create one, even if they weren't arranged the same way in your larger home.

3. Poor furniture placement.

This is related to, but goes beyond, creating a comfortable conversation area. Particularly in smaller spaces, people instinctively seem to push all the furniture up against the walls, thinking that will make the room look bigger. What it really does, however, is ensure that no one

Especially in limited space, a large sofa that juts out too far can obstruct the traffic pattern.

will be able to converse comfortably, and it also tends to make your room look as if you'd cleared the floor for dancing.

To avoid this, you can set a writing table perpendicular to a wall or arrange your conversation area in the center of the room. Just remember to leave enough open floor space so that you can cross the room comfortably without bumping your shins or walking between two people who are seated and trying to talk to each other.

An intimate u-shaped seating area helps keep both the conversation and the traffic flowing easily.

4. Creating a room that is off balance.

If you put all of your large, heavy pieces on one side of the room and the smaller, more delicate pieces on the other, your room won't be balanced, and you won't feel balanced when you're in it. A large or tall piece on one side needs to be balanced by something large or tall on the opposite wall. It needn't, however, be another big, heavy piece of furniture. It could be a tall plant or a vertical arrangement of artwork.

If you're taking or building a large wall unit or entertainment center, or a tall armoire, what will you be putting on the other side of the room? If it's a low sofa, you probably should hang a large painting over it to create the sense of balance that will help your eye move straight across, from one high point to the other, so that you feel more relaxed when you're in the room.

5. Creating a "roller coaster" effect.

When your seating or tables or lamps or artwork are of different heights, your eye will be forced to travel uncomfortably up and down around the room. Particularly in a smaller space, this can make you feel claustrophobic and dizzy.

If you have two tall wing chairs, for example, don't use them to complete a conversation area with a low sofa. Instead, put them in a corner to create a secondary seating area. Avoid using two end tables or two lamps of different heights, and if your built-ins don't go all the way up to the ceiling, be sure that they are in line with the tops of the door frames or other tall pieces in the room.

6. Creating a room that lacks cohesion.

You want your space to look pulled together because that will help you to feel more pulled together yourself. The simplest and surest way to do this is to use as many pairs as you can—pairs of chairs, tables, lamps, vases, even artwork. A cohesive room not only looks and feels

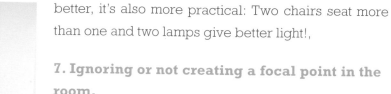

better, it's also more practical: Two chairs seat more than one and two lamps give better light!,

7. Ignoring or not creating a focal point in the room.

Particularly in a small space, it's important to give the eye something attractive to focus on. If you have a fireplace, arrange your seating so that it faces that focal point. If you have a great view, think about placing the sofa in front of the window to draw you and your visitors in. And if you don't have a ready-made focal point, you can create one by hanging a large, beautiful piece of art or a dramatic grouping above the sofa, where it's most likely to be visible when you walk into the room.

This entrance is functional but not aesthetically pulled together.

8. The improper use of artwork.

Using artwork properly means not hanging things too high and not scattering it all over the place, and always leaving at least one blank wall for the eye to rest on. It means using like framing materials and never hanging anything on a wall that is less than 36 inches wide.

All of these principles become even more important in a smaller space. When you're downsizing it's always better to err on the side of having too little rather than too much so that your space feels more open and airier. If you now have a collection of photos hanging on your wall, think about paring them down. Do you really

Adding a pair of vases and two pairs of pictures makes the same entry look more elegant.

This grouping of artwork, framed alike, brings the eye up and away from the heavy storage chest below.

Three retro posters hung above the sofa create a focal point where formerly there was none.

Hung at the correct height above a demi-lune chest, this round mirror enhances the entire vignette.

need eight shots of the bride or a half-dozen photos of the grandchildren taken on the same day? Be discriminating when considering what to hang on your walls; hang a variety of only the best.

Beyond that, when you do hang a grouping of prints or photos, be sure to place them no more than one and a half to three inches apart so that they have the most impact.

When you're deciding on height, I believe my "3-inch rule" works better than the old eye-level rule. It seems that it doesn't matter how tall you are—5 foot 3 or 6 foot 3—almost everyone hangs artwork too high. So, hold up the piece at the level you think it should be and then lower it 3 inches. Amazingly, I can guarantee that it will be in the right place.

9. The ineffective use of accessories.

The best advice I can give you about accessories is, now that you're downsizing and you have the opportunity, get rid of the junk! Go through your collections (we all have them) and discard the pieces that are broken, that you've outgrown, or that are not as good as others you've acquired more recently. And while you're at it, you can also let go of any guilt you may have about releasing this old stuff.

When you do display a collection that is important to you, keep all the pieces together in one place so that they will have the greatest impact and will be immediately recognizable as a collection rather than a scattering of "stuff."

Keep your collections in the room where they're most appropriate: antique canisters in the kitchen, teacups in the dining room, and so on. And remember—keep and use only the best!

10. Incorrect use of lighting.

In Chapter 6 I talk extensively about lighting, and which types of fixtures are most appropriate for which purpose. This is particularly important when you want to optimize your use of space and keep your home looking bright and welcoming at all times.

Some of the more common lighting mistakes are not using bulbs of the highest wattage your lamps will allow (especially in lamps that can handle three-way bulbs), not directing the light where it's needed, and making your room look smaller by using suspended fixtures such as large chandeliers rather than unobtrusive high hats or tracks in rooms with low ceilings.

Downsizing Your Home
WITH STYLE

Preparing for Change

AS WITH MANY THINGS in life, when it comes to moving, the more you plan and the better prepared you, the easier it will be. Being prepared means becoming as familiar as possible not only with what you've got but also with the home you'll be moving into, and that starts from the moment you sign the lease or go to contract and have access to the new space.

With any luck, you'll at least get a floor plan, but that's not enough.

What the Floor Plan Doesn't Tell You

Floor plans give you the overall measurements of each room, but they don't tell you how much space there is between a window and a door, between two windows, or from any opening to the adjacent corner.

They don't show you all the little zigs and zags, the places where the wall bumps out to accommodate the pipes. Nor do they indicate the height and width of the windows and doors; where random, odd-shaped windows are located on a particular wall; or even the height of the ceilings.

One of my clients made the mistake of not carefully measuring the space between an archway to her kitchen and the bay window in her new living room. As a result, when she moved her 7-foot-long entertainment unit from the large family room in her previous residence to her new, smaller home she found that instead of fitting perfectly as she'd thought it would, the unit jutted 6 inches into the open archway. As a result, she had to hire a carpenter to remove one section so the unit would fit on the wall without obstructing the traffic pattern.

Get Acquainted with Your New Space

Many factors can determine how much access you'll have to your new home. It may still be under construction; the previous tenants might still be living there with some or all of their furnishings; or it could be halfway across the country from where you're now living. But however much time you have, you'll need to make the most of it. So, before you access the space, make sure you have the following items:

- The floor plan
- A good, big tape measure
- A folder in which to keep fabric and paint swatches organized
- A digital camera
- A notebook and a pen
- A folding chair or two in case the space is completely empty. (You don't want to sit on the floor while assessing your space.)
- Photographs and measurements of *all* the furniture you now own. It's a good idea to write the measurements right on the backs of the photographs.

You may have decided in advance that a table or a bookcase is or isn't going to fit, but you may be surprised. So you need to measure *everything* (unless you really hate it and can't wait to get rid of it), and the photos will remind you of exactly what it looks like when you're far from home. You may *think* you're intimately familiar with every piece you own, but you'd be surprised how easy it is to forget the little table edge that sticks out farther than the legs or how big the arm of your sofa really is when it's not right there in front of you.

WHY THE RULE OF THUMB ISN'T GOOD ENOUGH

The term "rule of thumb" derives from the fact that the space between the first knuckle and the tip of your thumb is approximately one inch. But when you're trying to figure out what will fit where, approximate measurements just aren't good enough. When you "think" the desk will fit in the corner by the window and it turns out the space is even a fraction of an inch smaller than you thought, it may not be possible to "squeeze" in that rigid piece of wood. Furniture isn't like soft-sided luggage—you can't sit on it to cram in one more item.

Remember the old saying "Measure twice, cut once." But if you forget your tape measure, you can use a dollar bill: it is slightly more than 6 inches long.

TEN THINGS TO DO WHEN YOU GET THERE

1. Measure every single wall individually, no matter how small, and write it on your floor plan. The measurements should include:

This downsizer measured carefully to be sure that the bench she was bringing from her larger home would fit perfectly between an open door and a corner.

- The height and width of every opening: windows, doors, archways
- The measurement of every "space change": columns, sections of wall that jut out, indentations, curved walls, steps up to a platformed space or down into a sunken room, balconies, banisters, railings, central and baseboard heating units, radiators, and air conditioners
- The length of every flat wall
- The height of the ceilings, especially if there is a vaulted ceiling that angles from low to high at different points

2. Take pictures of every room from as many angles as possible. Start by shooting each room from every corner and then take some general photos that show as much of each room as possible. Remember, this place is new to you, and you won't be able to remember every nook and cranny when you are not there.

3. Figure out how much natural light you're going to have and where it will be coming from at different times of day. This will help to determine what kind of window treatments you will need and where you'll position the lighting.

4. Assess the condition of the ceiling, walls, and floors.

- Will you need to paint or paper?
- Do you want to add or remove built-ins, moldings, or chair rails?
- Will you need to sand, polyurethane, cover, regrout, or replace any of the flooring?
- Do you need to install overhead lighting or replace a fixture that is already installed?

5. Assess the doors and windows.

- Do any need to be replaced?
- Will any need new hardware?

6. Locate all the outlets for lights, telephone, and cable.

- Are there outdated, buzzing, or tired-looking dimmers with round knobs, or sleek new ones with adjustable settings?
- Will you need to add outlets on the floor and/or above the baseboards?

The sunny mirror provides a playful accent high on the wall in this bedroom with a vaulted ceiling.

- Will you need to add wall outlets for televisions or painting lights?
- If you are bringing track lighting from your previous home, will it need to be cut down or reconfigured?
- Do you need to add more spotlights? If so, where will you place them?
- Do you need to move the phone jack or the cable outlet or add a Wi-Fi connection? Mark all these locations on your floor plan as accurately as possible.

7. Investigate the windows and doors.

- Are the windows double-hung?
- Do they slide to one side?

HOW TO MEASURE AN "OPEN-PLAN" SPACE

In many instances you may have an open plan that includes more than one room. For example, you may not have separate living and dining rooms, but you'll still want to determine where one space ends "mentally" and the other begins. To do this, first measure the length of the entire long wall and then measure the shorter length that will be the designated dining area. This will help you to decide not only how much space you have for your living room pieces but also how much dining room furniture you'll have room for and how big the pieces can be.

The same idea applies to an open plan with an entrance area that flows into other rooms. In that case, measure the main wall of the foyer to find out if there is enough space for a chest, a cabinet, or a console you'd like to bring from your larger home. If not, there may be sufficient room for a small, round pedestal table or an oval cabinet that can be centered in the space to define the reception area and also serve as a place to put things down when you arrive home.

- Do they crank?
- How deep are they?
- Do they have an equal amount of wall space on either side?
- Does one side of any window go all the way to the corner of the wall?
- Are there double doors?
- Do the doors swing in or out to open?
- On which side do they open?
- Can the doors or their orientation be changed?
- Will you need to add 180-degree hinges that allow them to open all the way or remove any altogether in order to make room for your furniture? You don't want to put a piece of furniture where the door will bang into it every time it opens.

Brought together in a small entrance area, this armchair and table are both functional and attractive.

WHAT IF YOU DON'T GET A FLOOR PLAN?

You can always make your own "floor plan" simply by drawing the overall outline of each room and marking the locations of the windows, doors, columns, and other irregularities. Write the measurements on the drawing as if it were a floor plan. You won't need graph paper, since it won't matter if the drawing isn't exactly accurate—the measurements themselves will tell you what you need to know. Just be sure you don't leave anything out.

8. Check out the kitchen and bathrooms.

- Is there room for a small center island or a dining table in the kitchen?
- Are the appliances and countertops in good condition?
- What is the condition of the floor?
- Do the cabinets go all the way up to the ceiling or is there open space above them?
- Could the cabinets use a bit of sprucing up? Does the hardware need to be changed?
- Does the sink or faucet need to be changed?
- Is there sufficient light?
- Are the bathrooms in good shape?
- Is there wall or floor space for a cabinet or shelves?
- Are there cracks in the tiles?
- Does the tub/shower have clear glass doors?

Look at Chapter 8 for more on kitchens and bathrooms. Make notes of everything you see—the good, the bad, and the ugly—and indicate whether they are okay or need to be replaced.

9. Assess your closet space. No one ever has enough storage space, but when you're downsizing, the problem can be bigger (or smaller) than usual. In Chapter 4 I'll be giving you all kinds of tips on how to create extra storage, but for now you need to assess what you've got. Look inside every cabinet and closet.

- Are there shelves and an open area up above?
- Is there space between the clothing bars and the floor?
- Are there any little niches on the sides?
- Are double doors bifold, French, or sliding?
- Is it possible to replace wooden door insets with glass to provide your rooms with more light?

- Is there a coat closet? A linen closet? A utility closet or a pantry?
- Are there ways to make the closets you have more commodious, accessible, or useful? Can they be extended into an adjacent open space?

Write down whatever you see.

10. **Do** you have an attic, a basement, a one-, two-, or three-car garage? If so, make sure you investigate them.

- Is there enough space in the garage to create a separate room or a storage area for items other than your car?

Attics, basements, and garages, if you're lucky enough to have one or more of them, offer great possibilities for storage. Remember to insulate any of the areas where you plan to store furniture or personal items so that heat and moisture don't damage them. Unless your home is very old there will probably be electric outlets in the garage. If not, be sure to have a couple installed before you move in.

NOBODY HAS TOTAL RECALL

However good you think your memory is, it isn't! The last thing you want to do is get back to your current home and realize you forgot something you now need to know, especially if your new home is far from your present one. So write it all down, no matter how trivial or irrelevant the information may seem, and even if you think you'll remember all of it.

When You Get
Back Home

It is a good idea to enter all your measurements into your computer and to upload all the pictures you took. Create a file for your "move" photos and put the measurements adjacent to the photos so you'll have all the information you gathered accessible in one place.

You should also print hard copies of the photos with the measurements, because you're going to need those at your fingertips even when you're not at home.

Be Prepared!

Even if you were never a Boy Scout, Girl Scout, Cub Scout, or Brownie, this will now be your motto. And if you are not already a list keeper, this is probably an excellent time to become one.

One of my clients entered every detail of her move into her laptop and carried it with her wherever she went. Whether shopping, meeting with movers, or simply trying to figure out what she wanted to take to her storage facility, she had the facts and photos in front of her at all times. By eliminating most of the guesswork, she felt more confident and more relaxed.

In the next chapter I'll be talking about how to decide what to keep and what to part with, but there will certainly be things you'll need to buy. You never know when you're going to serendipitously come across something you think might be perfect, so, unless you're going to a dinner party or some other purely social event, there are certain items you need to have with you at all times:

1. **Your** floor plan

2. **Photos** and measurements of all the furniture and artwork you own

3. **Photos** and detailed measurements of your new space

4. **Paint** fan decks and samples

5. **Swatches** of existing fabrics you'll be taking with you

KEEPING COLOR IN MIND

When you're shopping, you need to have something with you in the color you want to match. You may think you have "a good eye for color," but why chance making a costly mistake? You can take a small pillow in the color you're using, but if you have a T-shirt, a sweater, or a scarf in the proper shade it will be easier to lug around than a pillow. But carry it; don't wear it. It can be hard to hold up against the item you're considering when you're wearing it.

Conversely, you can choose and take home an unlimited variety of paint samples in colors you think might be right. When you find the one that matches your draperies or upholstery or whatever it is you're trying to coordinate, tape it to an index card and carry that with you at all times.

6. **A digital** camera

7. **A small** tape measure

8. **A notebook** (better than a pad because it keeps things together and doesn't fall apart)

Before You Move In

It's psychologically important that you feel you're moving into a home that's fresh, clean, and welcoming rather than a space that looks worn and dirty or, even worse, like a construction site.

- Make sure all your electrical and cable outlets, phone jacks, and Wi-Fi connections are in place before you start to paint the walls. Otherwise, you might find that you need to channel some wiring inside a wall *after* your painter has finished.
- Make sure your walls are done—painted or wallpapered—*before* you begin to work on the floors to avoid drips on freshly sanded and polyurethaned wood or other flooring materials.
- Take care of any kitchen repairs, bathroom regrouting, or other "messy" jobs before the floors are completed.

As a general rule, I tell clients to work from big to small and high to low (ceiling fixtures and outlets, walls, windows, and finally floors). It's comparable to getting dressed: You shower and groom yourself first (get the "shell" of your home together—the lighting, paint, floors), then select your clothing (choose and arrange the furniture), and, finally, coordinate your jewelry (arrange the accessories).

2. What to Pack and What to Part With

COCO CHANEL HAS BEEN QUOTED as saying "Luxury must be comfortable; otherwise it's not luxury." And that is as true for your home as it is for your clothing. One way to make sure you're comfortable in your new home both physically and psychologically is to keep it clear of clutter.

A clutter-free room with tidy bookcases provides a visually restful living space.

CLEANING OUT IS A PROCESS OF DISCOVERY

If you've lived a long time with plenty of space, going through your things can become a trip down memory lane. Coming upon unfinished knitting projects or long-unused art supplies may inspire you to return to hobbies or brush up skills you've allowed to languish along the way. If so, you might want to create a knitting nook or find a place for your easel in your new home. Bring these activities back to prominence in your life by giving them a prominent place in your space.

If you're moving from a five-bedroom Tudor to a four-room condo, you'll be parting with a lot more than you pack. If your kids are married with kids of their own, and their bedrooms are still the way they left them when they went off to college, the decision to pitch their childhood furniture may not be too difficult. But wait—what if your grown son's bed can be used in a guest room? Will your daughter's computer desk work in your home office? Can you convert it into a writing table for your bedroom? If you're moving from one home to two, you'll also need to determine what goes where. Using color-coded stickers can help distinguish what is going where and which pieces are staying or going. Keeping too much might mean an unnecessary storage bill later on, but tossing too quickly can also be costly when you have to replace

The twin bed in this guest room was previously used in a child's bedroom.

something you had all along. The more thought you put into this process and the better organized you are from the start, the easier the whole move will be.

One thing you've really got going for you is that there is sure to be plenty to choose from. So, what you need to do is keep an open mind. In Chapter 5 we'll be talking in detail about repurposing your stuff—that is, using what you have in new and different ways. For the moment, however, consider the choices you'll be making if you now have a living room and a den, two or more bedrooms, an eat-in kitchen or a breakfast room, and a formal dining room. Something's going to have to go.

Downsizing may signify a purposeful change in lifestyle. You may want less formality and/or less upkeep. You may be moving from a cold climate to a warm one or vice versa. The way you're going to live as well as where will dictate the choices you make. For example, will you be doing more or less entertaining, and how will you do it—sit-down dinners, buffets, cocktails and hors d'oeuvres? Your current living room furniture may be too formal for your new home. Or maybe it's just too big. Would the den furniture be more appropriate and durable enough for use in your new living room? Or, conversely, if you're moving from the suburbs to the city, maybe it's the less formal furniture you'll be leaving behind. What about the master bedroom? Maybe the furniture from a second or third bedroom is less cumbersome or less beaten up—particularly if it was in a guest room that didn't get much wear and tear. Or a piece from the guest room may be useful in an entirely different way. If you had a large, formal dining room, do you have a table and chairs in the kitchen or breakfast room that are stylish and comfortable enough to use in your new, smaller dining area?

What to Consider—
Aesthetics, Comfort,
Condition, and Size

A lot of us keep things just because they're there and we're used to them. Or maybe you thought that if you changed one piece of furniture you'd have to change so many other things that just the thought was too exhausting. Well, now you're moving. This is your chance to replace

what you really don't like, rectify mistakes you made in the past, and start over. In fact, taking a "use it or lose it" approach might be helpful at this point in your life.

I'm not suggesting that you simply toss everything; my forte, after all, is to help you use what you have. But that means using the best of your furnishings as a foundation, and if you never liked your coffee table or if your sofa has never been comfortable, they're not going to change just because they have a new home. Or, if your mattress leaves you feeling like you slept on a roller coaster, this might just be the time to put it—and you—out of its misery. (As a general rule, you should buy a new mattress every seven to ten years.)

Asking yourself the six following questions as you're making your decisions can save you a lot of headache, heartache, and wallet-ache.

A refinished living room end table paired with a slipcovered ottoman on wheels now function as a small dressing table and seat in a master bedroom.

Newly upholstered and paired with a petite side table, this small-scale club chair fits proportionately into the conversation area and provides extra seating.

- Is it pleasing to me aesthetically and do I think it will continue to be pleasing in my new space?

- Is it comfortable and will it make me comfortable in my new home?

- Is it in good enough condition to warrant the expense of moving it? (If it needs fixing, but you love it, it may be worth it. Otherwise, this may be the time to let it go.)

- Is it versatile enough so that if it doesn't work in one room it will work in another?

- Is it of such great sentimental value that it will earn the space it requires?

- Does it fit and look good, and is it in proportion to the rest of the furniture in the room?

HOW TO MEASURE

When you're measuring a piece of furniture, you need to consider depth and height as well as length. It may fit along the wall but may still take up too much space. For example, an 83-inch-long sofa may not be too long, but if it's very deep it may overpower the room or obstruct a comfortable traffic pattern.

What to Keep—
Always, Sometimes,
and Never

There are certain basic rules about what to keep and what to leave behind that will help you with the selection process.

If you're merging two households, choices may become even more difficult because you're likely to have more than one of just about everything. In this situation it's even more important that you keep asking yourself the six essential questions on page 18.

And if you're merging households because you're merging your life with another person's, you each need to honor the other's feelings as well. Make a list of the things that are most meaningful to each of you, then consider which are in better condition and which will fit best. Be prepared to compromise.

Combining the desk and chair from "his" office with a sofa from "her" residence creates a home office/guest room.

ALWAYS KEEP

■ A sofa and two matching chairs—assuming the sofa is not too big

These pieces will create your conversation area wherever you go. Here's a handy rhyme to help you remember: "Keep a sofa with chairs or love seats in pairs."

f you have more than one sofa and must decide which one to take and which to leave, opt for the one with smaller, lower, softer arms— or perhaps, if your new space is seriously limited, one with no arms at all. The less space the arms take up, the more spacious your room will appear.

If you have only one sofa, or if you really love one more than the other but the arms are too big, an upholsterer can not only reupholster it but can also change the arms—and/or lower or straighten the back and reconfigure the pillows. Since you'll be making the pillows smaller, you even be able to use the fabric you already have. Making these changes will give you more space and will also make the piece look entirely new and different.

■ Armless upholstered "slipper" or dining chairs

These will fit almost anywhere, including in a bedroom or a foyer. Place two or three extra dining chairs side by side in the foyer, have one slipcover made to cover the whole group, and use it as a bench. You can still call one of the individual chairs back into service when necessary.

- Any chair or stool that swivels

Swivel chairs offer great flexibility, and are therefore very functional in a small space. They're particularly useful in rooms that have more than one focal point or more than one conversation area. Using swivel stools at the counter of a kitchen pass-through will also allow people to join the conversation on either side of the counter.

I n a smaller space, removing the skirts from chairs and sofas so that you can see the legs and floor underneath will create the impression of more space in the room.

Following this principle, Philippe Starck has actually designed a Lucite chair called a "ghost chair" (it comes with arms but I recommend the armless version) that you can see through so that the space seems more expansive. You can find it at the Museum of Modern Art or online from various Web sites.

- Beds less than 80 inches long or anything that opens into a bed

Twin beds, daybeds, high-risers, or trundle beds are particularly useful because they are multifunctional. With pillows at the back and bolsters on the ends to create arms, they serve as comfortable seating that can easily be transformed into extra sleeping space when needed, and with tailored slipcovers they look good in home offices.

- Anything that has storage in it

"Closed storage, closed storage, closed storage" is one of my mantras, and I hope it will become one of yours. Even if you have an old piece you don't really like, if it has closed storage, don't throw it out. You may be able to use it in a closet or put it in the garage, if you have one.

Pairs of table lamps and sofa pillows balance this U-shaped conversation area and provide both light and comfort. Note the end tables—trunks—that offer additional storage.

- Any piece that's on casters or small wheels

Again, the more flexibility furnishings have, the easier it is to arrange and use them. And, as an addendum to this point, putting plastic sliders, which come in many sizes and shapes and are available at most hardware and home improvement stores, under the legs of all your furniture when you are arranging it will make the pieces easier to move and will save your back.

- Pairs of lamps

Pairs of floor lamps, table lamps, or sconces will help to create a balanced look in any room.

- Ottomans

Ottomans can be separated from their chairs and used as additional seating, to create a U-shaped seating area, or, with a wood or metal tray on top, as a coffee table. Two chairs can even share a single ottoman to create a cozy conversation or reading area in a small space.

- Pedestal tables and drop-leaf tables

In a smaller space, one ottoman centered between two chairs saves room yet functions well.

Pedestal tables can be used in the dining room, living room, entrance foyer, kitchen, or bedroom; drop-leaf tables can stand against a wall with one or both leaves down and function as an entrance piece or an end table, and can be converted to provide additional surface area when necessary for eating, working, or entertaining.

- Pairs of end tables or bedside tables

Pairs create balance in any room.

- Any table or small cabinet with closed storage

Storage is always at a premium, and furniture pieces that provide it can be used in the living room or bedroom, or, with a larger top added, can serve as a desk or even a dining table. Changing the top on any piece of furniture will make it fresh and new and can also be a way to make it serve a new purpose. For example, you can put a marble top on a chest that might have been in an entrance hall and move it into the dining room to use as a server.

- Nesting tables or any furniture that stacks

Extra surfaces are always useful for both working and entertaining, and stackable furniture takes up very little room when it isn't in use.

- Bookcases and multisectioned entertainment units

Bookcases and entertainment units provide storage and display space not only for books but also for collections, audio and digital tapes, and photos in any room and can be reconfigured if necessary. If the bookcases are deep (more than the standard 12 inches) you can even store infrequently used files such as tax returns in back of the books, where they'll be out of sight but not out of mind and readily accessible when you need them.

In a room that is multifunctional, such as one that has an open plan combining entrance foyer, living room, and dining room, or a studio apartment, bookcases placed perpendicular to the walls at various points can be used to define each area. For example, two 7-foot-high bookcases placed at least 8 feet apart can separate living and dining spaces or even designate a "bedroom" area in an L-shaped or alcove studio apartment.

You might want to cover the back side of an open bookcase with burlap or cotton duck that matches the color of the unit and use the shelves facing the designated area to display appropriate items. A bookcase facing the dining area, for example, might hold serving pieces, extra dishes, or glasses. If the bookcase is facing the living room, the open shelves can be used to display a collection or a group of framed photographs. In a bedroom, the case could hold stacked, cloth-covered storage boxes, jewelry, perfume bottles, a clock radio, and, of course, books.

■ Benches

Besides functioning as seating in an entrance-way or at the foot of a bed, benches can hold books in a guest room, be stacked with matching boxes or storage baskets to hold supplies in a home office, be set on top of a server or buffet with books stacked in vertical piles both below and on top, and hold stacks of towels in a bathroom. Two small benches pushed together lengthwise can be used in the living room as a coffee table or set at the foot of a bed to hold

A bench in the entrance hall can be both decorative and a practical place to remove outdoor shoes and clothing.

throw pillows and coverlets at night. A bench can even be stored un-
derneath a console or a pair of open, leggy tables to be used for extra
seating when company comes.

■ Trunks

Trunks make great coffee tables while also providing storage. If you
have a sleep sofa in the living room or a combined office/guest room,
one large or two small trunks can be used as bedside tables that also
hold bedding. Or, you could set one on a platform with closed storage
and use it in the hall as an entrance piece, in the dining room as a
server, or behind the sofa as a table to hold a pair of lamps.

THE MOVABLE TRUNK

One client, who lived in a small studio apartment, had a trunk that she needed for storage. She also wanted to use it as a coffee table, but because her bed was a sleep sofa and the trunk was very heavy, she didn't think she'd be able to move it every night when she wanted to open the bed. I suggested that she put it on large casters (there are casters for both hard and carpeted floors), which would not only make it easy to move but also would raise it a couple of inches to a more standard coffee table height. The weight of its contents prevent the trunk from rolling whenever she put her feet up on it, and, with a bit of ingenuity, her problem was solved: Her trunk became multifunctional and she was delighted.

■ Track lighting

Tracks can be cut down, expanded, or reconfigured very easily by an
electrician to provide good general lighting in any room. New spot-
lights can also be mounted on an older track, if the track is in good
condition.

- Pendant lights

Pendant lights can be used in the kitchen, bathroom, or family room, or above a dining room buffet.

- Mirrors in good condition

Mirrors of all sizes and shapes can be cut down, hung horizontally instead of vertically (and vice versa), or used in place of artwork, and they help to make any room appear bigger and brighter. Furniture can be mirrored, or have old mirror replaced.

- Window coverings that will fit as they are or that can be cut down

If your new windows are smaller than your current ones, you can always cut down pleated shades or use the extra curtain fabric to upholster a small chair, to make throw pillows, to cover a transom window above a sliding door, or, in a bedroom, to upholster a head-board or a cornice and give any room a more pulled-together, cohesive look.

Think about using curtains in a different room—moving living room curtains to the bedroom, for instance—if that's where they fit best. In one instance, a client had a double window in the bedroom of her larger home that was covered by four panels of curtains—a heavier fabric for the two end panels with sheers in between. In her new, smaller home, the sheers went into the bedroom and the panels into the study, where they coordinated very well with the dark wood paneling.

Y ou may already have a chair upholstered in the same fabric as your
draperies. But what if that chair won't fit in your new space? Find a
smaller chair—a fully upholstered slipper chair or a wooden
armless chair with an upholstered seat/back—and upholster it in the
leftover curtain fabric. Or, if the curtains are in a bedroom, use the extra
fabric to make a pair of throw pillows, bolsters, an upholstered headboard,
or a bed skirt. Voilà! You've regained the cohesion you lost.

In addition, two chairs that are different styles but approximately the
same size and shape can be made to look as if they were meant for each
other if you upholster them in like fabrics. A contemporary fabric on a
traditional chair will change its look—and vice versa. So, simply by
reupholstering or slipcovering them, you'll be able to bring together pieces
that wouldn't otherwise have been compatible.

As an example of how well this can
work, one client who merged the furnishings
of her city apartment with the contents of
her beach house when she moved into one
much smaller house refinished a pair of
formal French armchairs in a lighter stain
and reupholstered them both in faux rattan
fabric in order to marry them with her
modern khaki-and-white-striped sofa.

Similarly, if you have two different
tables of the same scale and height, you can
have marble tops made for them, put
matching lamps on top, and hang matching

Using the same fabric on two chairs that are of the
same height and proportion but different styles
creates the effect of a pair.

matching lamps on top, and hang matching
art or objects on the wall above them to fool the eye and create the look of
a matched pair of end tables. Marble tops range in price based on size and
type. A small travertine top for a side table can cost approximately two
hundred dollars, whereas an exotic marble such as "blue spring" can cost
one and a half times that price.

A less expensive alternative is a plain, clear glass, polished-edge top
with smooth sides.

- Multifunctional appliances, such as a microwave/convection
  oven
- Under-cabinet appliances, such as a toaster oven, a coffeemaker, or a can opener
- Multifunctional office equipment, such as a combined four-in-
  one fax, printer, scanner, and copy machine

SOMETIMES KEEP

- Love seats

*If not in the living room, you might be able to use a love seat in an
entrance foyer or a family room, as a banquette in the dining area,
instead of a bench at the foot of your bed, or, possibly, in a home office
that isn't big enough for a full-size sofa. (If you have a pair or love seats,
always keep them.)*

- A small desk or writing table

*Small desks or tables can often be used in a kitchen, a guest room, or
an entrance foyer, or on a wall in a dining area.*

- Stools and footstools

With limited space, a writing table can take the place of a larger desk and offer a comfortable place to work on a laptop or write thank-you notes.

Two chairs across from the sofa and angled toward each other create a comfortable U-shaped seating area with an open traffic pattern for others to reach the cocktail table.

Stools can be placed in front of a kitchen pass-through counter to pro-vide informal seating, and footstools can provide a footrest or an extra seat if there is no room for a standard-sized ottoman.

- Club chairs

Small club chairs can add coziness to a living room, a family room, or a bedroom.

- Modular seating that is not too large

Sectional seating can be reconfigured to create a comfortable conver-sation area or even separated and, with one slipcovered, used in two different rooms.

THE FIVE BEST WAYS TO CONFIGURE A CONVERSATION AREA

Everybody I work with is stumped when it comes to reconfiguring their conversation areas when they move—especially to a smaller space.

The ultimate test of a properly designed conversation area is that everyone should be able to converse comfortably and no one should have to lift his or her bottom off the seat to reach the coffee table.

According to Dorothy Draper, one of the most influential and innovative interior designers of the first half of the twentieth century, "The more usable your coffee table is, the more livable your whole room will seem." I couldn't agree more! To be optimally "usable," your coffee table should be 15 to 18 inches from the sofa and a bit farther than that from the chairs. Standard coffee table height is 16 to 18 inches, although any small table that is 20 inches high can be used, too, providing it is not obstructing a television screen.

A U-shaped conversation area is the most intimate and comfortable for any living room or family room, regardless of its size, because it allows more people to be seated closer together and facing one another directly. Conversely, an L-shaped configuration is the least comfortable and creates what I call a "twist and shout" situation. You must twist your body to have an eye-to-eye conversation and you have to sit at the edge of your seat and raise your voice to be heard.

To create the ideal U-shaped arrangement, there are five possible configurations:

- Two chairs, one at each end of a sofa or a love seat, facing each other directly across a coffee table (if you have an L-shaped modular sofa, you'll need only one chair to complete this configuration; it's not a conventional U-shape, but it works)
- Two chairs angled toward each other across from the sofa and separated to leave an open traffic pattern between them
- Two chairs placed across from the sofa, close together and slightly angled toward each other, perhaps with a small table in between them
- Two chairs directly across from the sofa and squared off, with or without a small table in between the chairs
- Two love seats directly across from each other with two chairs at one end, slightly angled toward each other, or, in their place, an ottoman

- Recliners

If they're stylish and not large, recliners can be re-covered and moved from the den or the family room into the living room.

- End tables without storage

Second only to storage, surfaces are always desirable. In Chapter 5 you'll be learning about practical new ways to use end tables.

- Oversized headboards and footboards

Keep large bed components only if your new bedroom is large enough to accommodate them with enough room to walk comfortably around the foot of the bed.

- Baker's racks or any stylish metal rack

Baker's racks and similar pieces can be used to display a collection or plants, assuming you have enough space.

- Throw pillows

Pillows that are in good condition and coordinate with the color scheme of your new, smaller home can add comfort.

- Ceiling fans

Use ceiling fans only if they hug the ceiling and don't drop down too low, and only if the new ceiling will accommodate them. Ceiling fans look terrible on vaulted ceilings, for example, so consider the new space before you move a fan you won't be able to use.

- Outdoor furniture

Consider pieces of outdoor furniture that can function indoors, such as teak tables and/or folding chairs, wicker porch furniture, coordinated planters, or sculptures—particularly if you're moving to a warm, casual environment. One client had a wrought iron bench that she loved. She brought it indoors, added a pad and throw pillows, and put it in her foyer as an entrance piece.

NEVER KEEP

- Extraneous bric-a-brac
- Unloved books you'll never read a second time or unread books you never seem to get around to reading

Before this living room was rearranged, the glass coffee table, whose corners are dangerously sharp, put too much distance between the seats and prevented comfortable conversation.

Once the narrow coffee table was moved to replace the glass one, the conversation area became both more intimate and safer. Also, all furniture now sits on the rug.

- Framed posters you've had since college or artwork you no longer enjoy
- Small appliances or gadgets you haven't used in years (be realistic: If you haven't used them in a long time, you won't start now, and, in fact, you'll probably feel better and less encumbered without them)
- Anything of which you have "doubles"—from pots and pans to can openers and salt and pepper grinders

We all have a tendency to "replace" things and then hold on to the thing we're replacing "just in case." Now's the time to get rid of all the stuff that's worn out or not working properly— which is probably why you replaced it in the first place.

- Square or rectangular glass coffee tables with sharp, pointy corners

You need to be able to navigate through a room without having to bob and weave to avoid bumping into people or the furniture. One of the reasons I recommend oval or round coffee tables (and dining tables, for that matter) rather than square or rectangular ones with pointy corners is that they're easier to walk around without bruising your shins—and certainly safer if there are small children in the house. Although the normal "clearance" I recommend for a traffic pattern is 3 feet, the clearance in a conversation area is usually 15 to 24 inches, because everyone needs to be able to reach the table without getting up and to talk to one another without shouting—which is all the more reason, therefore, to choose a coffee table that facilitates rather than obstructs movement. Remember, if you must lift your bottom off of your chair in order to reach the coffee table, it is too far away.

- Any furniture that's worn, shabby, or not in good repair (unless it's an antique or something you love enough to have repaired)
- Oversized sofas (longer than 96 inches)

Even if you have enough wall space, unless the rooms in your new home are very large, an oversized sofa will be out of proportion and may overpower the room.

- Rugs that are worn (unless they're priceless Orientals) or too big for any of the rooms you are moving into
- Uncomfortable dining chairs
- Leggy plants or overgrown potted trees
- Old audio equipment and tapes or LPs you no longer use
- Mirrors that have damaged silvering
- Big grandfather clocks that have no sentimental value
- Unused pianos or other musical instruments
- Old, inexpensive ceiling fans
- Throw pillows and afghans that look dated
- Inexpensive metal torchiere lamps
- Ceiling fixtures that create a harsh glare
- Wall sconces that don't provide adequate task lighting
- Old pleated lamp shades
- Coat trees that take up space and almost always look messy

- Vertical blinds that are now outdated
- Old, unused baskets
- Worn-out bedding and table linens
- Tablecloths that will no longer fit your table
- Worn-out dish towels and pot holders
- Pots and pans that are stained or have lost their finish
- Dishes and glassware that are not in complete sets or are scratched
- Extra vases and candlesticks
- Personal tax records and receipt files that are more than seven years old
- Old piles of magazines (you know you'll never read them!)
- Unstable, wobbly bookcases

MIX AND MATCH

I'm a firm advocate of taking no more than two sets of china—one for every day and one for special occasions. When you're choosing which ones to take and which to part with, think about your table linens and place mats as well, and be sure that the linens you choose will go with both sets of china.

Honor Your Memories

Even though you need to weed through the tchotchkes you have collected over the years, you also need to honor key moments in your life by keeping those things that are most meaningful to you and that bring back good memories, even if they aren't necessarily the most useful or the most elegant things you own. You can't replace a memory once it's gone, so be thoughtful but not overzealous in your quest to get rid of stuff. When in doubt, ask yourself these three questions:

1. **When** is the last time I looked at this?

2. **Does** this represent a key moment or phase in my life?

3. **Do** I have another, more compact way of remembering this moment (e.g., a photograph)?

4. **Can** I display or use this differently or effectively in my smaller home?

5. **Will** I really miss this?

One interesting way to display collections that are meaningful (such as your children's baby shoes) but for which you no longer have surface space is to put them in Lucite boxes and hang them on the wall as art.

If you've lived in your home a long time you may have a strong emotional attachment to the place itself. One way to honor those feelings would be to take a little piece of home with you—a door that could be turned into a table or a desk or a couple of paving stones that could be laid into the floor or in a backsplash in the kitchen, for example. And if there's something very large that you can't take with you (even a tree that you've watched grow from a sapling), take a picture of it and hang it in your

This family took a photo of their front door to preserve a memory of the home they were leaving.

new home. Also, take photos of the house or apartment you are leaving, inside and out, to keep your memories fresh.

Good Buys

If you need a new, smaller sofa, check out Crate and Barrel's Bayside model, which is 80 inches long and comes with a washable slipcover, or its Ashton Sofa, which is 87 inches long, has stylish small arms, and is upholstered in stain-resistant cotton.

Or try Rowe Furniture's Mini Mod line of sofas, all of which are less than 80 inches long, some armless and with narrow arms. Many have a 1960s feel, and they come in many wood choices and hundreds of fabrics.

Carlyle Sofa offers the Chameleon armless sofa bed with two half-round ottomans that can be reconfigured several ways.

If you're looking for an unusual wall unit to use for storage or as a room divider, take a look at the Cubits shelving system by Design Within Reach. It's made of translucent or orange polypropylene and can be configured to suit your needs. Design Within Reach also offers a freestanding metal unit called the Sapien Bookcase that takes up very little space because the books stack horizontally. It comes in heights of either 60 or 80 inches and is 13.5 inches deep and wide.

For a trunk to use as a coffee table/storage unit check out Crate and Barrel's Taka Trunk. It has a small drawer to hold remote controls and opens from the sides, which means that you won't have to remove everything from the top every time you need to open it.

West Elm has a chocolate-stained wooden bench with a full-length storage compartment that can be used in an entranceway or at the foot of a bed.

Restoration Hardware makes the tufted Carlton Storage Bench, which is available in a wide range of fabrics.

Alsto's has an end table with nesting tables tucked inside so that they're not even visible, as well as other items of interest to the downsizer.

For a stylish, collapsible dining table you can store under your bed consider the Bobo Intriguing Objects table at ABC Carpet and Home. It's made of zinc and steel, seats six, and goes with modern décor or can be a fresh complement to a traditional room.

3. What to Do With What You Part With

SOMETIMES IT'S EASIER to part with your stuff if you know it's going to be put to good use or appreciated by someone else. And sometimes what you have is valuable enough to sell or auction instead of just tossing it in the local dump. Maybe your daughter has a daughter. Would she like to pass down some of the stuff from her childhood bedroom to her own child? What looks like kiddy leftovers to you may hold memories she'd like to share. If you do "donate" things to your children, however, be sure to give them a deadline for picking them up, and let them know that if they don't show up in time you're going to donate their stuff to a charity in their name.

LEND IT TO A FRIEND

If you're reluctant to let go of something entirely, you might consider letting someone else use it, with the understanding that you may be asking for it back at some time in the future. Rather than paying for storage, you'll be giving someone else the pleasure of using it—and saving yourself some money as well.

A number of years ago, I sold my country house and found that I had an extra upholstered chair and ottoman I didn't want to part with. My solution was to lend them to a good friend who had just bought a house. Until I need them again, she is using the cozy seating for reading and watching television in the master bedroom.

Have you been watching *Antiques Roadshow* and wondering if you're harboring a treasure? I'll let you know how to find reliable appraisers.

Small auction houses will also either buy things outright or take them on consignment. Or, you could sell them on eBay—and if you don't have the time to do that yourself, you can consign them to a local eBay salesperson. I'll tell you how to do that.

Is your garage full of gardening equipment you won't be using in the city? Why not hold a garage sale? After all, you've already sold the garage.

Charitable donations help you clean out while helping someone else, and you also get a nice tax deduction. And many charities not only pick up from your home but also provide a receipt that you can use for tax purposes. That said, however, don't try to donate things that are worn out or damaged. Most charities won't accept them, and if they're in such bad condition anyway, it's really time to toss them.

If you have furniture you can't sell or give away, you may be at a loss as to how to get rid of it. It's not always possible just to put it out with the garbage, particularly if it's large, heavy, or if you've got a lot. 1-800-Got-Junk has franchisees throughout the United States and in Canada that will take away anything for a fee.

How Much Is It Worth?

If you're selling or donating items to charity, you might want to know what they're worth before you dispose of them. If you're selling them you need to know what price you should be getting, and if you're donating them you'll need to know their value for tax purposes. I think it's particularly fulfilling to donate old books, CDs, and DVDs to a senior center or to give clothing to an organization that provides business attire to homeless women or welfare recipients who are looking for employment, such as Dress for Success (dressforsuccess.org) or The Women's Alliance (thewomensalliance.org).

To get an estimate of the value of your things you can contact the Appraisers Association of America (appraisersassoc.org), the American Society of Appraisers (appraisers.org), or the International Society of Appraisers (isa-appraisers.org). There are also appraisers who specialize in various categories, such as oil paintings, drawings, silver, old books, furniture, and china. If you have pieces you think are of value in a "specialist" category, you should try to locate an expert in your area.

You can, of course, call in a local dealer, but for obvious reasons, it may not be the best idea to get an estimate from the person who may also be the purchaser.

How to Sell It

TAG SALES, GARAGE SALES, AND YARD SALES

Traditionally, people have gotten rid of their personal "overstock"—whether they're moving or not—by having a tag, garage, or yard sale, and that's still a perfectly valid way to downsize what you no longer want or need, providing you live in a suburb, a rural area, and live in a warm climate or are doing this in the spring, summer, or fall. (Generally speaking, people won't be trekking around in the dead of winter to check out your potential bargains.) And in case you were wondering about the nomenclature, if it's held inside the home it's generally called a tag sale. If it's outdoors, it's a yard or garage sale. Wherever you hold yours and whatever you call it, be sure your sale is well advertised in advance. The last thing you want to do is go to the trouble of "tagging" all that stuff and then having to untag it again at the end of the day.

Place notices in supermarkets and schools and on online bulletin boards a week or two before the event. The day before your sale, put up signs on all street posts and in front of your house. Take a shopping bag with Scotch tape (for store windows), masking tape (for steel poles) and a stapler (for attaching things to wooden posts and trees). The most efficient way to accomplish this is to go with another person so that you can cover both sides of the street at once. (And be sure to post your signs facing in the direction that traffic will be coming from!)

The signs should say GREAT TAG SALE right at the top. Write or type your address and the start and finish times as well as the day(s) of your sale in big, bold letters, underlined in red so that the information is clearly visible to everyone driving by. Also, provide a rain date and be sure to say "no early birds" so that you don't have people ringing your doorbell while you're still in your robe sipping your coffee.

When we were newly married, my husband and I had our first tag sale at our country home on a beautiful autumn morning. Both of us had quite a bit of stuff from our single days, and we were ready to part with a lot of it.

We put out the tagged merchandise and some fresh apple cider for prospective customers and waited, along with two friends who had offered to help, hoping for a few people to show up. Well, at the stroke of 10 a.m. swarms of people walked through the front gate. We couldn't believe our eyes! We were swamped until 1 p.m., by which time most of our stuff had been sold. Everything moved so quickly we weren't even sure what some of the items had sold for. Had we known it was going to be such a whirlwind, we would have invited a few more friends over to assist us. From that experience we learned that in order to have a successful tag sale you need to be prepared.

Tag Sale Tips

- The items most likely to sell are antiques, collectibles, sterling silver and silver plates, small lamps and appliances, garden furniture and accessories, pottery, framed prints, black-and-white photographs, watercolors, and oil paintings, tools, sporting equipment, tapes and CDs, electronic equipment (in working order), and linens.
- The best day for a tag sale is Saturday, with Sunday as a backup rain date. The best seasons are spring through fall, from April through November.
- The more merchandise you have to sell, the better. If you don't think you have enough, ask a friend or a neighbor to partner with you.
- Whenever possible, use tags that attach with string rather than sticky price labels, which are difficult to remove.
- For electrical equipment and other mechanical items, indicate the size (such as "26-inch screen") and details (such as "in good working order") on the price label.

- Anything that's too big to fit in the buyer's car may be difficult to sell.
- Advertising in the local PennySaver is a good way to attract potential buyers.
- Save plastic grocery shopping bags for a couple of weeks so that you can wrap the things you sell.
- Borrow a few card tables to display your merchandise.
- Stock up on cardboard boxes for displaying old record albums and paperback books (spines up).
- As you organize what you want to sell, store all of the items in one room of your home or in your basement.
- Determine if your sale will be one, two, or three days long.
- Have a cash box and change for big bills (start off with a lot of singles).
- To get the most for what you have to sell, be sure that everything you display has been dusted or cleaned.
- Display like items, such as toys and books, together.
- Be sure that people can walk comfortably from table to table and easily see what you've displayed.
- Have festive music playing to create an upbeat, fun atmosphere.
- Assign family members or friends to make sure that no one makes off with an item that hasn't been paid for—or that wasn't for sale in the first place.
- Situate the payment table next to the exit.
- Price things to sell! The object is to get rid of them, not to get rich.

AUCTIONS

If you have a number of valuable things that you no longer want or need, you may decide to consign them to an auction house for sale. If you've ever watched *Cash in the Attic* on BBC America, you know that it's possible to realize a sizable return on a wide variety of collectibles and furnishings at small local auctions.

The usual procedure is that an appraiser will value the items you want to put up for auction and determine the prices they're likely to bring. Some auction houses also have free walk-in consignment days when appraisers will evaluate a limited number of pieces and accept certain items for upcoming auctions. Either way, the appraiser will let you know the date of the next appropriate auction and give you a consignment contract to sign. The contract will list the items you're consigning and the estimated sale price as well as the reserve, which is the minimum price for which the item can be sold. If any of your items don't meet their reserve, they will remain unsold, which means they'll be going home with you. The contract will also state the percentage of the sale price the auction house will take as commission.

Generally speaking, it will be about two months from the time your items are accepted to the time they're sold. The auction house uses this time to photograph the pieces and create a catalogue for the sale. Most auction houses have trucking services that, for a fee, will pick up pieces you cannot deliver yourself. There is also generally a Web site on which sellers can track the items they've consigned.

Sellers receive their payments four to five weeks after the auction. Pieces that do not sell can be rescheduled for another auction or picked up after you pay a small service fee.

Doyle New York (doylenewyork.com) has regional appraisal days in Darien and Glastonbury, Connecticut; Washington, D.C.; Scottsdale, Arizona, and other areas. Doyle will also buy fine pieces of art and furniture outright.

EBAY

In addition to tag sales, eBay has become perhaps the most universally popular method of selling an almost endless variety of stuff. You can certainly do it yourself, but if you're in the midst of getting ready to move, you may be too busy and have too many other things on your mind.

If that's the case, you can call upon a designated eBay "seller" who will come in and assess what you have and then, for a fee, do the selling for you. The seller will generally require a minimum bid of $150 per item, will usually get a commission of 30 percent, and won't pick up lots worth less than $2,000 total. Since you can put a minimum bid on the items you offer, you don't have to sell it for less than you think it's worth. But that also means that if it doesn't reach its minimum, you'll be getting it back. Or, for a small fee, it can be put up at another auction with a lower minimum.

Several years ago I used an eBay service when it was time to clear out the contents of a storage unit that contained things my family no longer needed. After sorting through everything, I provided a list of items to the firm, which sent someone to pick up the merchandise. After consulting with me by telephone, the seller established the price for each item and then notified me by e-mail when the auctions were posted. Afterward, I received a printout and a check for everything that had sold. Because my first experience was positive, I have turned to this firm twice more to sell other pieces.

OTHER SALES OUTLETS

- **Craig's List (craigslist.com):** To use Craig's List, look for your city, then go to "create posting," "for sale." Make a list including a title or headline, a description and price of each item, and an expiration date. You can also post digital pictures of the items. You will be assigned a number and an anonymous e-mail address to which the potential buyer will reply.
- **Local Newspapers:** Advertising particular pieces in the local newspaper can be a good way to attract buyers who are

looking specifically for what you're selling. I would not, however, suggest advertising a "household" sale in general, as that kind of open invitation is likely to attract more browsers (or curiosity seekers, or worse) than legitimate buyers. I'd also suggest that you don't include your address in the ad. If you put in only your phone number, those who are truly interested will have to call you to find out where to go. That will allow you the opportunity to get the caller's name, and, if you wish, to phone the person back in order to get a sense of whether or not he or she is "legitimate." And you won't be advertising your home address to everyone who happens to read the paper.

- **Dorm or Student Center Bulletin Boards:** College kids need things for their dorm rooms or apartments and are always looking for bargains. (This would also be a good way to recruit extra man power if you need it for a tag sale.)

- **Consignment Stores:** Consignment shops are generally for high-end items that are in good condition. You and the owner of the shop will determine what to charge, and the shop will generally keep half of what you get for the piece. You can authorize the consignee to drop the price after a certain period of time. The shop owner will also determine the length of time for which he will keep it; if it isn't sold within the specified time period, you'll be notified to pick it up. If you don't, the shop will do-

Consignment shops may be interested in selling your finer pieces, such as this antique Buddha.

donate it to charity. Any money you receive is considered income and must be declared on your income tax.

Since she downsized to a smaller home, one of the interior refiners with my firm has maintained a working relationship with a consignment shop in her town. As she acquires new accessories or tires of pieces she's had for a long time, she takes them to the shop to be sold. As a result, her home has remained clutter free, and she continues to get "extra" spending money for her shopping sprees at the estate sales she loves to go to on weekends.

- **Vintage Stores:** If you have vintage furniture, accessories, or clothing, go to a specialized store that has a greater market for these items and where you are, therefore, likely to get a better price.

- **Thrift Shops:** Thrift stores a run by charitable organizations in order to raise money. They will sell donated secondhand items, but unlike consignment stores, which pay you a percentage of the sale price of each item, they will give you one receipt for all the items you donate to use for tax purposes.

- **Estate Sales:** The way an estate sale works is that you sign a contract with a company that sends people to tag everything being sold. Check with the Better Business Bureau and interview at least two companies with good ratings that will not charge you for the initial meeting and that provide you with references. And check to make sure the one you choose has an up-to-date business license and insurance. Once you sign the contract, you're committed to the sale. These companies won't do just a room or a few items; they really want to deal with the entire house.

Be sure the company uses a master pricing list that requires buyers to consult with them about each piece rather than tagging each item and allowing potential buyers to browse independently. And make certain that you place items you do not want to sell in a closed-off area where browsers will not see them.

An estate sale can last two or three days, and many companies reserve the first day for antique dealers exclusively.

The price of these services varies based on your location and the size of your home but are usually a percentage of the gross.

If you live in a condo or a cooperative apartment building, before holding any kind of sale, check to see that there are no restrictions. But even if you live in a house, most towns require permits to run sales and some may also have parking restrictions. Check with the town or village hall. The information is often available online.

4. The Truth about Storage— You Can Never Have Enough

Storage in Your New Home

PERHAPS BECAUSE I've always lived in New York City, where living space is notoriously at a premium, I'm constantly thinking about new and different ways to create additional storage for my clients, even when they don't bring up the subject themselves. And it appears to be one of the basic facts of life wherever you live: No one ever has enough closed storage space. Even if you're home is very large, you just seem to grow into whatever space you have. So if you're now living with an attic, a basement, and a garage and are moving to a place that has only one or none of these, storage is bound to be one of your primary concerns. To compound the problem, the smaller your space is, the less cluttered it should be. Therefore, what may have looked fine in your larger home might just create visual chaos in your new one.

One of the things I'm going to teach you is the addendum to my "closed storage, closed storage, closed storage" mantra: Air equals potential storage. You'll learn to look up, down, and all around to find places you may never have thought of to store what you have either in or out of sight, because any niche or empty space, no matter what size or shape, can be used to create additional storage.

Reassess Your Closet Space

If you've been following my advice, when you assessed your new home you checked out the closets and noted whether there were shelves above the clothes bars and/or space underneath. With that in mind, here are some tips for making the closets you have more useful and commodious.

- If there isn't already a shelf above the hanging bar, have one built. And if there is a lot of space above a single shelf, check to see if there is room to build another one above it. Even if the shelves are too high to be easily accessible on a daily basis, they can certainly store out-of-season sweaters, pants, hats, scarves, gloves, and even shoes. Plus, there are all kinds of plastic containers that can be stacked to store these items while

One of the best tips I can give you—and the one you may thank me for the most—is to get all the new storage areas and built-in pieces in your new home completed before you move. I guarantee that it will make your move a lot less stressful because you'll be able to unpack your things and put them where they belong immediately instead of having them standing around in cartons until their permanent homes are ready to receive them.

The wall-to-wall, built-in storage cabinet in this dining room was installed prior to the downsizer's move, enabling her to unpack and organize her things as soon as she arrived in her new home. (Note: The armless chairs and round, glass-topped table make the downsized space feel airy and tranquil.)

keeping them clean, neat, and visible. Just be sure that the containers you buy are all one uniform style so that your closet looks elegant instead of disordered.

In one instance I suggested that a client create a separate door above the door frame of her closet so that she would have easy access to the highest shelves, where she stored luggage and out-of-season clothing.

If there is sufficient space below the hanging clothing (or even to the side, below your shorter items), you may be able to fit in a small chest or bureau. Or consider an additional hanging bar for slacks or shirts if you have space below the existing pole.

- The insides of doors that swing open can be used to hang shoe racks, belt holders, hooks, and tie racks.

- If you have a walk-in closet, to utilize all the available vertical space, you can buy a rolling step stool or a small ladder that will allow you easy access to even the highest shelves.

- When closet space is limited it might be worthwhile to call upon a custom-closet expert to configure the space you have so that it fits your particular needs. Not only will this make your life easier, but if you own your home, it will also add to the resale value. For customized closet resources, see "Good Buys" at the end of this chapter.

- A freestanding cupboard or armoire set perpendicular to a wall can also act as a room divider, separating the space in a shared bedroom or in a living room with a home office space. If there are windows at only one end of the room, the space between the cupboard and the ceiling will allow light to filter through. (You can also mount a bulletin board on the back of the piece.)

Create a Closet

Do you have a room with a corner niche that's not being used? Maybe next to a column that's enclosing the pipes? If so, you might want to have a carpenter build a closet to your specifications and paint it the same color as your walls. Many of the older buildings in Europe and the UK weren't built with closets. All the closets and cupboards are freestanding or built in. Consider bringing a little bit of old Europe into your home.

One of my clients had moved from a house to a two-bedroom condo with two small children and told me she was "going crazy" because she had so little storage space. When I arrived and was able to assess what she had, I found four separate areas where she could create additional built-in storage, each of which would be different enough from the others so that her open-plan living, dining, and TV areas wouldn't look like a giant storage unit.

In the dining area, we built in a bench with sliding doors that was 18 inches high and ran across the entire short wall so that all the interior storage was accessible from the front. The client already had a very small hutch that didn't hold much, so we stood it on top of the new bench, anchored it to the wall, and put baskets between the legs of the hutch for even more storage.

A curtained-off niche with lots of shelving creates a closet where there was none.

The second built-in was created in an existing niche between two French doors on the outer living room wall. It has closed storage at the top and bottom, with three open shelves in the middle to hold a collection of family photos.

The third place we created more storage was on the opposite wall, where there had been a very large (90-inch-wide) opening to the bedroom hallway. We extended one side wall and left a smaller, yet comfortable, 35-inch passageway to the bedrooms. The newly extended wall would accommodate another floor-to-ceiling storage unit with double doors opening on the hallway side. Once it was painted to match the rest of the wall, the new built-in looked as if it had always been there.

And finally, in the TV area there was a wall approximately 8 feet across on which we hung a television with storage units both above and below it. The family's video equipment would sit on top of the lower cabinet (beneath the wall-mounted TV) and the children's toys would be stored inside, where they could reach them easily. The upper, wall-mounted cabinet could be used to store other items.

The moral of this story is that there's always room to create additional storage if you just look around and use your imagination.

Bookcases and Built-ins

One well-designed built-in with both open and closed storage can hold an immense amount of stuff, from your TV and audio equipment to your home computer, books, a file cabinet, linens, liquor, dishes, and glassware.

It may be a personal pet peeve of mine, but I hate those tall metal, wooden, or plastic freestanding towers that hold discs. No matter what their style, they generally look messy, and they take up valuable floor space. If you have one or more, this is your chance to bid them a fond farewell. If possible, store everything out of sight in a cabinet, on a closet shelf, or in a drawer.

If you're having a built-in custom designed, be sure to make a list of all the things you would like to house in it before you meet with your carpenter so that you can inform him or her of what you intend to use it for. And be sure that you use all the vertical space available. Standard built-ins are 7 feet high, but you might consider building yours all the way to the ceiling in order to get the maximum amount of storage.

One of my clients called me a few years after she'd downsized because she'd run out of storage space. The moment I walked through the door of her town house I realized that all the space above the 5-foot-high, 8-foot-wide wall unit in her living room was going to waste. With nearly 9-foot-high ceilings, she had the opportunity to create more storage directly above the unit. Taking my advice, she hired a carpenter to build a 3-foot-high addition in the same veneer and running the entire length of the unit so that, when it was done, it looked as if it had always been there. Aside from giving her

A small desk next to an open bookcase creates visual chaos.

Once the bookcase is replaced with a closed cabinet, the room feels more tranquil.

This built-in uses most of the floor-to-ceiling space to maximize closed storage.

plenty of new storage space, the new section is removable so that if she ever sells her home she can take both the bottom and top sections to another space and use the pieces either together or separately.

If you have an entertainment center that doesn't quite fit in your new space, yet you need more storage, consider how it might be re-configured. Many of these pieces are sectional and can, therefore, be removed and made larger or smaller. Pieces that don't fit in their present configuration might actually be used as separate units in different locations or reconfigured with the addition of doors; a new, matching, connecting piece; or a lower piece to use as a desk or dressing table.

Bookshelves with closed cabinets underneath can be built from floor to ceiling and even go over the top of a doorway and down the other side to create an entire wall of open and closed storage that looks

C lients of mine had a large entertainment unit with closed cabinets on either side and, in between, eight glass shelves that held books and collections with a column down the middle. By removing the central column (which had supported the shelves but was not otherwise needed) and replacing the glass shelves with three wooden ones near the top, they were able to make room for a 50-inch LCD television with a media rack below for all their other electronics, and still have a lot of space on the shelves above for their books. Not only did their twenty-year-old unit now accommodate their new television, thereby saving the space it would have required elsewhere in the room, but the changes also gave it an entirely new and modern look.

Another client had a low media cabinet that was meant to hold electronic equipment with a television on top. Since she was no longer using it for that purpose, I suggested that she have a cushion made for the top and use it as a bench with closed storage underneath.

Removing a vertical wood column and glass shelves from the center section of this entertainment unit made space for a large new television, audio equipment, and bookshelves.

Bookcases built floor-to-ceiling and even over the doorway provide a lot of open storage space without cutting down on the size of the room. A library ladder will allow you to access even the topmost shelves. Remember, always line up books flush to edge of shelf for a library look.

extremely cohesive and doesn't cut down very much on the size of the room. Most bookcases are only 12 inches deep and the closed storage on the bottom can be anywhere from 12 to 20 inches, depending upon the size of the room.

Use the open shelves not only for books but also for collections, photos all framed in the same material, or other decorative objects. Create a balanced arrangement by keeping like items on the same level. For example, place all hardcover books on top shelves, all framed photos on the center shelves, and all paperback books on bottom shelves. If you don't need constant access to all of the paperbacks, you can organize two rows, one behind the other. Most important, be sure these are books you really need to keep. If not, you can donate them to a hospital, a senior center, or your local library.

As for the closed space on the bottom of the unit, the choice is yours. Use it for whatever suits your needs—photo albums, small electronic equipment, or Christmas decorations. Remember, no one but you needs to know what's in there.

EVERYONE NEEDS A JUNK DRAWER

You probably have one now. It may hold a variety of small tools, Scotch tape, string, rubber bands, little pieces broken off from something you can't identify. Now's the time to clean it out—but assume that you'll be starting a new one in your new home, and designate a place for it. If you want to take it a step further, you can splurge on a drawer organizer, but, organized or not, it's better to have a utility drawer than a messy space!

Secret Places
for Extra Storage

- Cushioned window seats that open—from the top or the front or at the ends—or built in, under-the-window radiator or air-conditioning units that run from wall to wall and have storage at either end (if you're having a window seat custom built, it will make your life easier if you ask the carpenter to make doors or drawers that open from the front so that you won't have to lift the seat cushion every time you want to access the items that are stored underneath)
- Benches that open
- End tables or coffee tables with drawers and/or cabinets underneath

A cushioned window seat serves many purposes: It can hide heating and air-conditioning units; serve as additional, comfortable seating; and provide closed storage as well.

- A stack of vintage leather or wicker suitcases that can serve as an end table and also provide hidden storage for files
- A new or old flat-topped steamer trunk that can function as a coffee table
- All kinds of wicker, canvas, or metal baskets
- Ottomans with tops that open
- Niches behind curtains or sliding shoji screens
- Behind a freestanding screen with trees on either end
- Headboards with storage
- Wall partitions with built-in storage
- Large, decorative, hinged wooden boxes that can serve as tabletops
- Hollow freestanding pedestals or some that are under tabletops

BE CREATIVE

Columns add architectural detail and break up the space in an open-plan home. Have them made hollow, with shelves or a door on one side, and use them for extra storage. Just remember to paint them the same color as the walls so that they "disappear into the woodwork."

- Empty pieces of luggage for storing out-of-season clothing
- Behind a sofa and end table that have been pushed against a wall
- Under the bed (see "Good Buys" at the end of this chapter for resources for closed containers that will slide under the bed as well as "bed risers" that lift your bed so that more will fit under it); you can even use an extra-long bed skirt (have one made or add a border to a standard one) to keep what's stored out of sight.

- Captain's or platform beds with drawers that can hold a great deal of stuff (to avoid bumps and bruises, just be sure the platform doesn't extend beyond the mattress).

Baskets and Boxes Galore

Baskets these days are not just for flowers or knitting. Boxes are made of a lot more than cardboard. Both come in every conceivable shape, size, material, and color, and can be used next to a chair or a bed or under a bench or a table to hold any number of items you don't want to leave exposed to clutter up your space. Line them up in bookcases to create a uniform storage system or stack them in a home office to hold supplies or extra paper for your printer.

I don't generally recommend putting anything on the top of a built-in or a bookcase, but if you have one that's only 5 feet high (as opposed to the standard 7 feet) you could neatly stack solid matching baskets or boxes on top to hide a multitude of stored items in plain sight. The same would be true of a 7-foot piece set between a pair of taller windows. Stacking a few attractive and uniform storage boxes on top of the piece

The open space under a console holds baskets of incoming and outgoing newspapers. The hinged box on top holds keys, mail, and dry cleaning receipts.

would not only provide another spot to keep things but would also fill the negative space between the windows, creating a straight line for the eye to move across instead of a visually uncomfortable rollercoaster effect.

See "Good Buys" at the end of this chapter for places to purchase all kinds of baskets and boxes.

Office Equipment for the Home

File cabinets, both traditional and lateral, come in all kinds of wood finishes and a variety of metals with hardware that will blend right in with your other furniture, even in the living room. Many don't even look like file cabinets, and if you don't already have any, you can buy old ones from companies that sell used office furniture. In addition to holding files, they're a good place to store your office supplies—or anything at all, including extra linens.

We all know about using file cabinets with a board across the top as a desk, but you can also use them as tables at either end of a sleep sofa in a den or an office-cum–guest room or between a pair of chairs.

One of my clients had a kitchen with a long, empty wall that was lacking counter space. My solution was to bring in two black metal file cabinets and position them back to back, with one side against the wall. I then arranged her cookbooks on top, straight across, with her blender at one end and her coffeemaker at the other, serving as bookends. Now she is able to use and access both file cabinets, her cookbooks are within easy reach, the countertops have been freed up for other uses, and the black cabinets tie in to some of the other black accents in her kitchen.

Off-Site Storage

By now you've "edited" your belongings, but there may be pieces you're still not ready to give up, even though they don't have a place in your new downsized home. You may be making an interim move because you're not yet ready to buy; you may want to get a feel for your new neighborhood before you decide whether it's going to be your permanent home; you may be waiting for a change in the real estate market; or you may simply be keeping things because you think your children will want or need them when they acquire their first home.

Whatever the reason, there are ways to make sure that your storage experience will be as trouble free, practical, and economical as possible.

Before It Leaves Home

MAKE SURE YOU REMEMBER IT AND CAN FIND IT AGAIN

Whatever it is you're going to store, you need to take its picture and its measurements before you send it on its way. Photos help you remember what Aunt Maggie looks like even though you haven't seen her in years, and the same is true for your furniture and accessories. I know you think you'll remember every one of your well-loved belongings, but memories fade, and these reminders will let you know—without making an unnecessary trip to the facility—whether that sideboard you put in storage really will go with the new dining table you bought and whether it really is as big (or as small) as you seem to remember.

If you're storing things in cartons, you need to number each carton and label it as specifically as possible. Then make a list (on paper, on your computer, or both) of what's in each numbered box. By doing this, if you do have to retrieve something, you won't be wasting time and injuring your back moving boxes around to find the one you're looking for. And be sure to stack your boxes in numbered order, too.

MAKE SURE IT DOESN'T GET BROKEN OR DAMAGED

Going to your storage unit and discovering that your grandmother's china is smashed to smithereens or that the legs on your Chippendale table are cracked can be extremely upsetting on two counts—the broken piece or pieces may not be replaceable, and you'll have been spending good money to store something that's no longer usable. To avoid those kinds of unpleasant surprises, make sure that the items you store have been properly packed and prepared.

- Waxing your wood pieces, even if the storage facility you're using is climate controlled, will help to prevent them from drying out and will also protect them from dampness.
- If you're removing screws or hardware from furniture, put the pieces in ziplock bags and tape it to the underside of or inside the piece so that it doesn't get lost. (Be sure to use tape that can be easily removed.)
- Remove the legs of furniture whenever possible (many simply unscrew) so that they don't get broken.
- Wrap all electronic equipment in bubble wrap and tape down moving parts.
- If you still have record albums (and some may actually be valuable these days), stand them vertically in cartons so that they don't warp.

- Bubble-wrap small, breakable items and store them in the drawers of a dresser (if you're storing one). Then tape the drawers shut.
- Wrap lamp shades in paper or bubble wrap and stack them on top of one another in a single box.
- Get the right boxes for the job. There are special boxes for artwork and others for crystal or china. Your moving and/or storage company will usually provide the proper supplies (for a price). Using recycled supermarket cartons isn't going to be cost effective if your precious possessions are broken.
- Pack heavy items in small boxes and light things together in large boxes to make lifting easier.

Choose the Storage That's Right for You

Storage is storage, right? Wrong! Actually, there are two basic kinds of storage facilities: container or long-term storage and mini- or self-storage.

Container/Long-term Storage: Long-term storage is generally meant for large pieces of furniture that you won't need to access for some time. Moving companies often have their own long-term facilities and will quote storage rates as well as moving rates if you ask for them.

When you put things in long-term storage you should know that they may not be easily accessible. You will probably have to call in advance if you need access to your unit, and the hours of access may be limited.

Be sure to ask about access before your stuff gets hauled off so that you aren't unpleasantly surprised, as was one of my clients who didn't realize that her furniture was going to be shrink-wrapped and put on pallets and that to access it she would have to make an appointment between 8 a.m. and 12 noon and hire two men at $20 per hour each to help her.

Mini-/Self-Storage: Self-storage is usually used for smaller items that can be packed in cartons or even clothing that can be stored on racks. Most cities have several mini-storage facilities that are easy to get to and easy to access. You rent a locker or a room (they are available in several sizes), receive your own key, and can access the unit to inspect, remove, or add to your stored items whenever you choose.

This kind of storage is generally more expensive than the less accessible long-term units, so you'll need to determine in advance how much that easy access is worth or whether it's really necessary for you.

Good Buys

HOME STORAGE

In the past ten years an entire industry has grown up around the need people have to keep more stuff in less space. Many of these companies didn't even exist twenty years ago. Here are some to check out.

For organizing:
The Container Store
Organized Living

For customized closets:
California Closets

Closets By Design

Easy Closets

Poliform USA

Stacks and Stacks

Clos-ette (Holistic Organizational Design) designs closets in New
York and Florida and sells closet accessories online

For all kinds of storage:

Attic Dek (for plastic storage racks)

Closet World (for all storage, including for the garage and the
basement)

Lowe's (storage for every room in the house)

Home Depot/Expo (for closet organizing products and storage)

Home Focus (for indoor and outdoor organization and storage)

KangaRoom Storage (for collapsible storage boxes of various
kinds)

PackMate (for closet storage bags)

Rakks (for glass, metal, and wooden shelving units)

For good storage pieces:

One of my all-time favorite pieces is the Nexus Storage Cube
from Design Within Reach, which can serve as a stool, an
ottoman, or a side table. It's made of leather, and the top can
be flipped over to expose a wooden tray and the storage
space. Best of all, it's on casters so that it can be moved easily.

A number of furniture companies, including The Door Store, offer
less expensive versions of this cube in wood or microfiber.

Home Decorators Collection has a line of leather furniture with all
kinds of storage options, including leather suitcases in various
sizes that actually function as file cabinets.

Crate and Barrel sells attractive woven rattan ottomans that open
for storage and can be used as extra seating.

Alsto's has bed risers that lift the bed so that there's more storage space underneath.

OFF-SITE STORAGE

Door to Door Storage and Moving, located in several states, will bring an entire storage container to your home on a flatbed truck and leave it on your lawn or in some other spot that's easy for you to access. You pack the container yourself and they pick it up and take it to a storage facility. Each container is 5 x 8 x 7 feet and holds up to a room and a half of furniture; you can ask for as many containers as you'll need. You'll be given a key and can access your container(s) if you call the facility in advance. This may be a good choice if you're packing up your entire household and your new home will not be immediately available to you. At least you'll know that all of your belongings will be together in one place.

FlatRate Moving, with several facilities in Maryland, New Jersey, California, and Florida as well as in New York City, Washington, D.C., and Las Vegas, is reputed to be a good, reliable moving company and also to have good, clean storage facilities.

Moving.bz will direct you to mini-storage sites in your area and provide other information about moving.

5. Repurpose Your Stuff

THE KEY TO USING what you have in a different space is to give up your preconceived ideas of where it should go and what it should do. Once you get over the notion that each piece has to be used in the same room that it was in your previous home and for the same purpose, you'll be able to keep more of what you love—including your hard-earned cash. Repurposing breaks down into two basic strategies: Changing where and/or how you use something, or changing the size, shape, or color of something to make it work differently—and perhaps even more effectively—in your new space.

For example, one downsizing couple I worked with is now using a small painted cabinet that had been in the bedroom of their larger home in their new bathroom, where it works perfectly as a storage cabinet for their towels and also provides a surface for their tissue box and a flowering plant.

If you think it through in advance and look at things with new eyes, the transformation will be seamless and your pieces will look as if the way they are is the way they always were.

Move It Around

We've already discussed the possibility that your den furniture may fit better and be more appropriate in your new living room or that your kitchen table may be moving to the dining area, but there are many more ways to think about using individual pieces differently or in different rooms.

One client, who had moved from a 3,000-square-foot house to a 1,600-square-foot town house, no longer had a den or a formal dining room. We took the leaves out of her dining table and moved it into the living room to create a new dining area, put the buffet in the hall as an entrance piece, and removed the wide center section of her hutch so that she could use the two end pieces with a smaller stand in the middle to hold her TV. Finally, we put the sofa that had come from her former den, along with a floor lamp, into the small dining area to create a den space. She would be purchasing another matching lamp for the other end of the sofa and a small round coffee table to put in front of it. She now has a small, cozy den and can still put the leaves back into the dining table to seat more people when she has guests.

- **Pedestal tables** can be used as dining tables. In fact, in a small space, using a pedestal table will take up less room, will provide more leg room so that you can seat more people at either end, and will allow you to push the chairs farther underneath the table when they're not in use. Or, put one in your kitchen if there isn't enough room for a standard-size breakfast table. A low pedestal table can be used as a coffee table or between two chairs in a family room or a living room; a tall one will look great in the center of an entrance area and will serve as a convenient place to drop things when you come through the door. You can also use them as bedside tables in a small guest room.

- **Bedside tables** with closed storage can be used as end tables in the living room. If your current end tables have long legs and no room for storage, and you have an extra set of bedside tables that do, consider moving them to the living room. And, of course, the opposite is also true. If you have an extra set of end tables with storage, they can be moved to a bedroom as bedside tables.

  In one home we did something unconventional that worked really well: We moved a pair of leggy end tables from the living room of the previous home into the master bedroom of the new home to be used as bedside tables. We then placed two smaller, espresso-stained mini-chests under the end tables. "Stacking" the tables gave the couple more surface space than they would have had with just the smaller pieces but also preserved the storage provided by the chests.

- **Large side tables** can be used in a bedroom or home office as a writing table or a desk. You can even add a larger top to provide more work space. A pair of these tables can be placed against a wall and separated so that there is sufficient space for a kneehole opening in the center. With the addition of one long wood or marble top and access to an electrical outlet, the new long surface will accommodate everything you need for a functional home office.

- **Large dining tables** do not always have to be positioned in the center of a room. Many of my clients are surprised when I suggest that they do not have to replace a big table; instead, they can simply position it against a long wall or under a window in their smaller home and tuck in the chairs at either end and on one long side. (This is also a great time to consider using recessed or track lighting that does not restrict the placement of the dining table and provides the dining area with good general illumination.)

- **Any long, narrow table** such as a Parsons table or an Asian prayer table (these come in various wood stains and are usually less than 20 inches deep) can be used as a sideboard in a small dining room. A table that ran along the back of your sofa but will no longer fit into your living room can be used as a console in your new entrance or behind your bed as a shelf to hold your clock radio, books, and phone if you do not have the space for end tables (and assuming there is enough room to walk around the foot of the bed comfortably).

PARTNERING ACROSS A PARSONS TABLE

Clients of mine had a small study they wanted to share as an office, but it wasn't really big enough to hold two desks. My solution was to position a Parsons-style table they already owned with one end of the table abutting the wall and a low bookcase flanking it on either side. Now they can sit facing each other across the table, and because we put it on casters, they can also roll the table out to use as an extension to their dining table when they need extra seating for guests.

- **A drop leaf table (with one leaf folded down) or a demi-lune pedestal table** can be used in a small entryway as a place to keep keys and drop your mail when you come in, or in a small dining area or kitchen with two chairs as a dining table. It can even be used as a computer table if there isn't room for a desk.

- **A bench** that may have been in the foyer might work at the foot of the bed to hold covers or throw pillows you remove at night. Or use it in a child's or grandchild's room with stuffed animals or toys on top and underneath and within easy reach. If a young child is sleeping over, the bench can also be placed along the side of the bed to prevent the child from falling out.

- **Extra dining chairs** can be slipcovered and used to flank a chest in the hallway, creating a pair, at a desk in the home office, or at a writing table in the bedroom. The slipcovers can then be removed and the "extras" called into service when there are guests and you need additional seating. Or you can put four in the kitchen and four in the dining area. Slipcover those that will be used in the kitchen with practical, washable cotton fabric.

- **Armless upholstered slipper chairs** can be used instead of larger club chairs to create a comfortable U-shaped conversation area. If they don't match the sofa, you can have slipcovers made in a coordinating fabric instead of having them reupholstered. Armless slipper chairs can also be pushed together side by side to create a "love seat" and, if you wish, can be slipcovered to look like one piece.

- **A small club chair and a matching ottoman** can be used to flank the coffee table in a living room or a den to create the effect of a pair when there is not enough space for two upholstered club chairs or if you want to avoid having to purchase a second chair. Reunite the two pieces when you're

This handsome bureau now serves as a bar with ample closed storage beneath.

An extra chest may provide more storage space than a small TV stand.

reading or watching television and separate them when you have guests.

■ **A small chest or bureau** can move from a bedroom to the living room. With a tray on top it will make an attractive bar and also provide some much-needed storage. Or it can be used in an entrance foyer with the addition of a marble top to give it a more elegant look.

If your dining room isn't big enough to hold a buffet or a server, a small chest with a stone, glass, or metal top will provide a practical surface to hold extra food and drink. For one of my clients, I suggested that a special wooden piece be made to fit across the open top drawer of her dining room "bureau/ server." Now, when the top drawer is pulled open, the wooden piece rests securely on it, creating additional serving space while protecting the table linens that are stored inside the drawer.

A small bureau or chest can also be used in place of a TV stand. Put the television on top of the piece or mount it on the wall above, depending upon the available surface space. Place the rest of your electronic equipment on top or underneath. Or, if possible, have glass panels installed on the front of the cabinet so that the equipment can be stored inside and operated by remote control.)

- **A sideboard** that no longer fits in the new, smaller dining room may work in the living room instead. That way you'll still have someplace to keep extra serving pieces, dishes, and glassware that may not fit in the kitchen cabinets and aren't used every day.

- **An armoire**, with the doors on or off, can be used to house a television.
- **Twin beds** that were formerly used in one or two of your kids' rooms can be used in a second bedroom or a home office to create a guest room. Configure them lengthwise along one wall, side by side with a small chest or bedside table between them, or in a L-shape, depending on the size and shape of the room. Alternatively, you can push them together to create a king-size bed for the master bedroom.
- **Rugs** that were formerly used in a living room conversation area but don't fit in your new, smaller space can be used in a bedroom or study, where they may give the effect of wall-to-wall carpeting and also provide better acoustics. Even if the rug is smaller, it can be laid under the bed so that the ends are

exposed on either side, giving you a nice, soft place to step on when you get out of bed.

If your new conversation area is too small for a busy, patterned rug, but the rug is the right size, try this trick: Flip the rug over. The reverse side is lighter and flatter, which makes the whole rug less conspicuous and more modern but still elegant. This works well for rugs that are a bit worn on the top side, too.

■ **A small crystal chandelier** that may have been in a hallway can hang in your new dining room, over the island or breakfast table in the kitchen, or in the bathroom. Even if your other fixtures are sleek and modern, it can be fun to bring in a more traditional piece to offset and soften the more modern stuff.

A small crystal chandelier becomes a whimsical accent when paired with modern dining room furniture.

- **A group of small, framed mirrors** that may have been in different rooms can be brought together and hung in a group as artwork.
- **A small decorative screen** can stand in front a hearth when the fireplace is not in use—so long as you remember to move it whenever you light the fire. You can also hang or stand it behind a bed to serve as a headboard.

If you miss your garden, or your indoor plants are taking up too much space and you have a nonworking or unused fireplace, consider making it your designated indoor garden. Put small plants in similar containers on the mantel, and larger ones both inside the opening and on the hearth. If the area you're using doesn't get sufficient natural light, you can purchase a plant light (sold at any garden center) to spotlight your greenery.

Make It Fit

You'd be surprised how adaptable some of your stuff really is. Legs can be cut down, removed, or changed; carpets recycled as area rugs; mirrors rotated; pieces taken apart and used in different rooms.

- **A tall cabinet** may be too high if your ceilings are low or it may simply seem out of balance in a smaller space. If it's on legs, the legs may be screwed on and easily removed, or they could be cut down or cut off. Check it out before you decide to leave the piece behind, especially if it has closed storage.

For long-term flexibility, especially when downsizing, stick with a bed that does not have a footboard.

One of my clients had a tall, glass-fronted, antique cabinet that she loved and wanted to use in her new home. But the piece was too tall, or so she thought. When we inspected it, we realized that, in fact, the cabinet was in three separate pieces stacked upon one another. We took off the carved top piece, and voilà, the cabinet, although less ornate, was still beautiful and now usable in her downsized home.

■ **A bed** with both a headboard and a footboard may not fit in your new bedroom. In many instances, however, the footboard and side rails are removable, which means you'll be able to salvage a useful piece by using just the headboard, and you'll avoid the unnecessary expense of replacing it. (This is one of the reasons I advise my clients to buy beds without footboards if they are planning to move in less than five or seven years. No matter what size your next home may be, footboards inevitably create problems with traffic patterns).

In addition, if you have an upholstered headboard that ties in with your drapes or other upholstered furniture but is too high and looks out of proportion in your new, smaller bedroom, you can often cut it down and, if necessary, set it in a wood frame that coordinates with the other wood furniture in the room.

Another creative option, if there's no room for any headboard at all, is to have a head-

This triangular gold-leaf frame was hung above the bed when the downsized bedroom was deemed too small for a conventional headboard.

board painted or stenciled on the wall itself. You might also get a relatively flat (no more than 3 or 4 inches deep) upholstered headboard and attach it to the wall directly above the mattress. That way, the bed will still be flat against the wall and the headboard won't impinge on your floor space. Yet another option is to hang a piece of art or a mirror above the bed in place of a headboard.

FOUR-POSTERS AND CANOPIES—MAKING THEM FIT

f you're lucky enough to have a great, big bedroom, keeping your canopy bed won't be a problem. But if it's going to obstruct the traffic pattern or make you feel claustrophobic, there are ways to downsize your bed and still preserve its style.

If your ceiling is not very high, you can remove the canopy and leave the posts, or, if the posts unscrew, you can have them cut down and turned into small wooden finials that will make the whole bed feel as if it's taking up less space. Another option, if you prefer, would be to cut down the legs of the bed and leave the canopy intact.

- **Solid wool, nylon, or sisal carpeting** that's in good shape can be cut down to use as one or more area rugs or as runners on either side of the bed. The two newly created runners can also be sewn together at the short ends to create one runner for a long hallway.

  Once you've cut down your carpet you can have it finished with a self-binding or you can have a contrasting cotton or tapestry border added to pull in one of the colors in your upholstery. This will give your "old" carpet the look of something entirely new and create additional cohesion in the room. If you

The accent tapes on these white wood venetian blinds match the wall color and give the room a cohesive look.

have a leather sofa or just like a modern look, you can even have the border made from the same color leather. (This also works, of course, to enlarge a rug that's too small.)

■ **Blinds** can be cut down to fit smaller windows or, if both your old and new windows are standard size and your blinds have cotton accent tapes, you can simply change the color of the tapes to coordinate with a new color scheme. (Don't bother to reuse passé vertical blinds.)

■ **Curtains** that are too long can be rehemmed. If your new windows are narrower, curtains can be made narrower too. Use the leftover fabric to create a custom look by having throw pillows, bolsters, and a dust ruffle made for your bed, or to slipcover or upholster a small chair.

C urtains should be one of two lengths, to the windowsill or to the floor, not flapping somewhere in no-man's—or -woman's!—land. So, if you had floor-length curtains in your larger home and your new windows are taller or have a built-in window seat or radiator cover, or furniture underneath that is as wide or wider than that window, cut the curtains down to windowsill length. For taller windows you can also add a border at the bottom for a more modern, panel look and additional length. (And remember to use the new accent fabric elsewhere in the room to give the space a cohesive look.) For wider windows, a panel of coordinated fabric can be added to the existing curtains to broaden them. In a smallish space, curtains shouldn't be billowing on the floor in any case. As a rule of thumb, the smaller the room, the more tailored your window treatments should be, so keep them neat and not puddled.

- **A vertical mirror** can be hung horizontally if your ceilings are low. If the room is small but the ceilings are high, hang a horizontal mirror vertically. And if the mirror is big and framed, consider leaning it against a wall, either sitting directly on the floor or on top of a piece of furniture.

- **Hanging fixtures**, whether on poles or chains, can often made to hug the ceiling more closely.

- **A sectional sofa** can be reconfigured or one or two pieces removed so that it works your new, smaller space. Consider adding a small table between two of the formerly attached modular sections to provide a surface for a lamp and drinking glasses.

- Use three armless pieces to create an armless sofa.
- Put two corner pieces together to create a love seat.
- Use an armless piece and an ottoman to make a chaise.
- Put three or four armless pieces (with or without an ottoman) around a round coffee table to make an intimate conversation area.
- Place two armless pieces together, across from two other armless pieces, to create the effect of two love seats.
- Use two armless pieces as individual slipper chairs, two corner pieces to make a love seat (or two corners and an armless middle piece to make a sofa), and an ottoman. Arrange the chairs perpendicular to either end of the sofa or the love seat and place the ottoman across from it with a coffee table in the center to create a comfortable conversation area

Before the modular seating was reconfigured, this L-shaped conversation area was awkward and uncomfortable.

After a quick adjustment, the U-shaped configuration provides a comfortable place to chat, read, or watch television.

An extra bookcase found a new home when it was turned on its side to conceal messy wires and a small file cabinet in this home office.

- **A fireplace mantel** that takes up too much space can be removed, leaving just the hearth, or it can be replaced with a narrow shelf to hold decorative accessories.
- **A pair of low bookcases** can be stacked on top of each other and anchored to the wall to save floor space.
- **Tall bookcases** can be turned on their sides on the floor. Stack tall books lying flat and use other sections to display collectibles. You can place the bookcase itself in front of a desk that's facing into the room to disguise the exposed wires from the computer or other electronic equipment.

BOOKCASES DON'T HAVE TO HOLD BOOKS

Bookcases can hold books in combination with other objects or be used for another purpose entirely. They are a great way to display a collection, a group of like-framed family photos, or framed artwork for which you have no wall space.

One client had a beautiful marquetry bookcase and no place (she thought) to use it in her new home, so I suggested that she move it into her dining room and use it to display pieces of china—like a breakfront without the glass doors.

- **An end table** that's too large—particularly if it's round or oval—may just make the perfect coffee table. Or pair it with a chair and use it as an alternative writing table or a place to set up your laptop. If necessary, add a new, larger top.
- **Pairs of wide end tables or chests with closed storage** turned sideways, so that their backs are against the sides of the sofa and the drawers are facing out to either side, take up less room, and you'll still be able to use the storage space.

You can transform an end table into a coffee table by cutting it off at the knees, so to speak. The standard height for a coffee table is 16 to 18 inches (although if it is frequently used to serve food it can be as high as 20 inches), whereas an end table is generally 24 to 30 inches high. If you don't consider yourself "handy" you may want to get someone to do this for you. And if you're going to put the table on wheels (I believe that making furniture easily moveable is always a big plus), remember to buy the casters first and consider the height they will add when you're deciding how much of the leg to cut off. Try to match the metal finish on the wheels—chrome or brass—to other metals on the piece itself or other pieces in the room, and be sure to get those that are appropriate for your type of floor (i.e., either carpet of hard flooring).

GOOD BUY

The Service Caster Corporation in West Reading, Pennsylvania, offers more than 40,000 caster and wheel combinations.

6. Camouflage and Sleight of Hand

WHAT YOU DO with the "shell"—the walls, floors, and ceilings—as well as what you put into your home can make the space appear either cramped and overstuffed or airy, open, and comfortably roomy.

Paint It Larger

Think of "dressing" your home as you dress yourself. You probably know that when you dress yourself in a single solid color from head to toe you look longer and leaner than when your top is a different color from your skirt or pants. Also, if your skirt, hose, and shoes are all one color, your legs always look longer. You can apply those same principles to your home.

One clothing trick you might want to think twice about, however, is dressing all in black. I know we all think we look thinner in black, but that's because dark colors make things look smaller—whether it's your body or your rooms. If you have a small den or TV room that isn't used much in the daytime, it may be cozy-chic to paint the walls dark burgundy or chocolate brown with white trim. I have done this myself, but as a general rule, smaller rooms will look bigger and brighter when the walls and ceilings are light. And if you do choose to go with a darker color on your walls, be sure to add lots of pure white elsewhere—in the fabrics, window treatments, and art—so that you don't wind up feeling as if you're living in a cave. Another caveat: Be sure you plan to live in that home for a while so that you don't have to repaint (at least two coats!) in order to make the space more appealing to a buyer.

WHEN WHITEWASHING WORKS

Quite a few homes have one brick wall in the living room. If the room is small and does not get a lot of natural light, you might consider whitewashing the brick, which will preserve the texture while making the room appear bigger, brighter, and more cheerful.

Particularly in a smaller home, it's important to have a unified color scheme throughout. Every room doesn't have to be exactly the same color, but having at least one color, if not two, running throughout will tie things together and keep your rooms from looking chopped up. If the living room, dining area, and kitchen are built on an open plan, paint them all the same color, and, if you like, choose one wall—perhaps in the dining area—to paint a contrasting accent color.

White or off-white paints are always safe, but if you simply must have color, consider a banana with gray undertones, icy gray-blue, greige (gray-beige), toast, mushroom, light green-blue, or a silvery green washable matte paint. Any of these hues will look sophisticated and won't deter potential buyers who might be put off by bright or bold-colored paint. Pastels and primary colors look dated and—if you're even thinking about resale now or in the near future—may adversely affect the value of your home when you move. You can, however, add a glaze that will add interest to your walls, reflect light, and brighten the look of the entire space. If you love bright colors, save them for your accessories. Brightly colored throw pillows, artwork, or even a collection of glass or ceramics will add a delicious splash of color to any room.

Keep the walls neutral and use brightly colored accessories to liven things up.

Build Your Own
Wall

Even in an open-plan space, you may want to create more of a division between certain areas. Clients of mine, for example, wanted to separate their dining niche from the central living area so that it wasn't immediately visible when you walked in the front door. To do that without making the space seem even smaller, we built a floor-to-ceiling wall of ribbed glass blocks, leaving a 3-foot passage to walk through. Not only did the wall conceal both the dining area and the kitchen but it also looked very stylish, and the glass let in the light from the living room windows. Glass blocks are a particularly good and classic option when you're creating a separate space that won't have any windows, but you can build walls or half walls from other materials as well, such as Sheetrock, wood, stone or river rock, or built-in bookcases, to alter the way spaces are defined or give the illusion of separate rooms in an open plan home.

Another option would be to use a piece of furniture, such as a cabinet with a finished back, placed perpendicular to the wall, to define the space. If, for example, it separates the dining area from the entrance hall, the front of the cabinet could be facing the dining space and the closed storage used to house dishes, glassware, or serving pieces. With a couple of accessories on top you'll have completely changed the dynamic of the space.

Another creative way to build a semipermanent wall is to hang wooden venetian blinds from the ceiling to separate a section of the room—to create a small home office space, for example. When your workday is done and the blinds are down and closed, you won't be able to see from one space to the other, which means that your office will be out of sight and out of mind.

Or, in an L-shaped studio, you could put a Japanese rice-paper-and-wood shoji screen across the opening to create a separate bedroom. When you're home alone you can leave it open; slide it shut when you have company. Shoji screen companies can be found in the yellow pages of most major cities.

Here are some other items you can use to define spaces in an open-plan home.

- Two open or closed bookcases (one on either wall, with an opening/traffic pattern in center)
- One or two matching, freestanding screens
- Louvered, bifold doors on one or two walls
- Two large trees or pedestals holding branch-filled urns on opposite walls to divide the space
- Built-in sliding doors with clear or frosted glass panels
- Curtains hung from the ceiling that can be left open or pulled shut

Camouflage Tips for Making Rooms Bigger

- If the room has many doors, which create architectural chop, painting all the doors the same color as the walls will keep the eye moving and make the room feel larger. This is especially true in foyers that have doors of various styles—such as double front doors, sliders, and bifolds—all in the same area.
- Even if your room has a chair rail, paint the walls the same color above and below the rail. Alternatively, you could remove the chair rail entirely to eliminate the break in the wall.

We painted these bifold doors the same color as the walls and added the white trim across the bottom to carry out the line of the baseboard molding.

- Don't be afraid to paint paneling to make the room look larger (unless, of course, it is carved and truly beautiful)
- If you live in an older home that has picture molding, to make the molding less conspicuous, you can either paint the molding and wall above it white, or paint the molding and walls the same color all the way up to the ceiling. Then paint just the ceiling white. For an even cleaner, more modern look, you can also have your painter or contractor remove the molding entirely.
- Always keep some extra paint on hand so that if you find a perfect piece at an estate or consignment sale you can paint it to match what you already have and make it blend into the wall.
- If there are windows of different sizes or shapes or doors of different heights, painting the walls and the trim all the same color will help camouflage the disparities.

HOW MUCH DETAIL DO YOU NEED?

Like chair rails and picture moldings, crown molding will add architectural detail to a straight flat ceiling, and, in a traditional style home. It medallions for ceiling fans or light fixtures add interest, but if you're trying to keep the eye moving to make your space appear larger, remember that the less you break up the space the bigger it will seem.

- If you have built-in bookcases or an entertainment unit, painting them the same color as the walls will help them fade into the background. And, if you're having new ones built, painted pieces are much less expensive than either hardwood or veneer.

- A dark, overpowering armoire can be painted white or to match the color of the wall or refinished in a light-colored stain to appear lighter and less imposing.

- Painting the molding and ceilings white will make your ceilings look higher—use semigloss for the trim and flat paint for the ceilings (which aren't going to get walked on or bumped into). As a general rule, the shinier the paint, the easier it is to clean, which is why it is best to paint both kitchens and bathrooms entirely in satin or semigloss.

Do You Love Wallpaper?

If you really must have wallpaper, be aware that the busier the paper, the smaller the room will appear and the more visual chaos it will create. And again, if you may be reselling rather than staying indefinitely, the choice between living with or removing your English country flowers or Chinese pagodas from the walls could discourage potential buyers. There are, however, many more neutral types of wallpaper, including linen, nubby, ribbed, faux leather, crocodile, or python, all of which are textured rather than patterned. Another option, particularly if you have sound issues, would be to "upholster" a wall in corduroy, linen, or wool (depending on the climate), all of which are great sound absorbers. And if your ceilings are low, vertical striped wallpaper will also add height. Choosing one of these options might just satisfy your papering urge while preserving your sense of peace and won't adversely impact a potential resale. And if you do decide to use paper, you should definitely paint the ceiling white and all the trim white or the lightest shade that is in the wallpaper.

If you still have that urge to wallpaper, and you have a traditional home, you can paper the inside back wall of a bookcase or a niche. Just be sure to choose a paper that ties in with the color scheme of the room.

Windows Are Part of the Walls

When downsizing, the main idea is, of course, to expand the space you have, not to make it look smaller and choppier. One way to do that is to keep your window coverings neat and trim and within the frame of the window. Even if you had dramatic, flowing draperies in your previous home, using a lot of fabric that takes up wall space on either side of the window and/or puddles on the floor will probably not be appropriate in your new, smaller rooms.

If you install a fabric treatment, remember that light solid colors or tone-on-tone stripes are visually soothing, while busy, bold prints are less restful to the eye. Simple, sheer tergal (a synthetic silk look-alike), raw or smooth silk, linen, or cotton-linen curtains that match the walls are all good choices.

Simple tension rods are the easiest, least conspicuous, and least expensive way to hang curtains inside the frame. You can also use more ornate poles with finials and rings, hung just above the window or on the top of the frame itself. Just be sure to select a metal finish or a wood stain that coordinates or blends with other elements in your room.

Some other options for inside (the frame)-mounted window treatment that can be used alone or in combination with curtains, a valance, or a cornice are shutters—either traditional style or the larger and more modern plantation style in white or wood stain—pleated shades, 1-to-3-inch wooden blinds in a variety of finishes, matchstick blinds or bamboo shades, and "silhouette" style sheer vane shades. If you have standard size windows, many of these can be bought ready-made. As with the hardware you choose, the color or stain of the blinds, shutters, or shades will be less obtrusive and leave your space feeling more open the more it blends with the color of your walls.

Fool the Eye

One exception to the "within the frame" rule would be if the tops of your windows are lower than the tops of your doors. In this instance, hanging the curtain rod above the window frame and at the same level as the top of the doors will fool the eye and make the room feel more balanced. The same rule applies if you have windows of different heights within the same room. If you hang all the curtains at the same level, the windows will appear to be of uniform height.

Another way to fool the eye is to cover a triple window with a single blind or shape, which will look less choppy and make the space seem larger than it would if you hung three separate window coverings.

And, if you're lucky enough to have a wonderful private view, you might not need any window coverings at all. Instead, you could leave them bare and have a reflective window film applied directly to the inside of the windows to cut the glare, save energy, and protect your furniture and fabrics. (And, if you live in an area where hurricanes are a consideration, window films also offer greater protection from flying objects in high winds.) 3M and other companies manufacture the films.

To bring in more light or simply to add architectural interest, any standard-size window can be enlarged or sometimes made into a French door, even if it doesn't open and doesn't lead anywhere.

What about the Floors?

As with walls, the smaller and more open your space is, the more important it is to keep the flooring uniform throughout. And light-colored floors will make your home look more open and airy. Wood or bamboo flooring and porcelain or carpet tiles are all practical choices. Porcelain tiles don't require resealing the way marble does, and they're also stronger and more durable. To give your space a wider, more expansive appearance, install the tiles on the diagonal.

If wood floor, **Engineered wood flooring** is affordable and strong—more durable than hardwood—and doesn't require sanding or polyure-thaning. (Conversely, it can't be sanded if it's scratched or you want to change the color.)

Bamboo wood flooring is beautiful, available in many different styles

Tiles laid on a diagonal make this narrow kitchen appear wider than it really is.

and finishes, and eco-friendly because bamboo is an easily renewable resource.

A traditional hardwood floor is lovely, but I don't recommend it in the kitchen, where the inevitable spills would necessitate more care and frequent polyurethaning.

Carpet tiles are very affordable and particularly practical for family rooms, high-traffic areas, offices, and children's bedrooms or playrooms. The tiles are made of nylon, wool, or hemp and come in a broad range of colors and styles. And, best of all, you can install a whole room in two hours without using glue.

Area rugs not only warm up the room, they also help to tie together your color scheme and define the living room conversation area. In an open-plan home, however, I recommend having only one rug, in the living room area. Even if the colors are compatible, multiple rugs will chop up the space and tend to fight with one another.

To define a conversation area, you generally have three sizes to choose from: 6 × 9, 8 × 10, and 9 × 12. Any of these sizes will look good and function well in most rooms; it's just a matter of personal preference. And keep in mind that the bigger the rug, the more expensive it will be. So, if your budget as well as your space is limited, don't hesitate to purchase a smaller rug.

A 6 × 9 rug would be centered under the coffee table, and the front legs of the seating might or might not be on it, either of which is okay. An 8 × 10 rug would fit under the front legs of the chairs and the sofa, and a 9 ×12 would go underneath all of the seating in the entire area.

One place I always urge clients *not* to use a rug is under the dining table. Unless you have a formal dining room that's used only for holiday dinners or family get-togethers, a rug under a table is simply a crumb-catcher that will require constant cleaning and maintenance. Stick with a wood, tile, or stone floor that is easy to clean.

Another absolute no-no is putting an area rug on top of wall-to-wall carpeting. To me, this is no different from wearing a jacket on top of a f you want to define the dining area without using a rug, you can stain the wood floor under the table a different color or have an artist define it with a painted border and protect it with a couple of coats of polyurethane. You can, of course, do the same with the conversation area in the living room. Just keep in mind that these are semipermanent solutions, so be absolutely sure before you spend money that this is something you'll be comfortable living with for a long time.

coat—redundant and unnecessary. Not only is the pile-up (pun intended!) a trip hazard, it also looks bulky and always makes me think that the rug is hiding a stain. So don't even put a small (2 × 3) rug on top of the carpet next to your bed. The carpet alone will give you a soft, cozy place to put down your feet and the rug will just make the space look choppy.

The benefit of a rug, besides softening the floor, is that it anchors and defines the space. That's why it's a good idea to use one under a conversation area. Conversely, the main reason wall-to-wall carpeting is effective, besides its acoustical benefits, is that it makes a room appear larger and more open with an uninterrupted visual flow. Nylon is stain resistant and wool is easy to clean, so both are good options. When it comes to wall-to-wall carpeting, however, you need to be aware that in a smaller space your traffic pattern will be more confined and that carpet in heavily trafficked areas will show wear and tear sooner than that in the other areas. For that reason, I don't recommend wall-to-wall carpeting (or any rug at all) in frequently walked-on areas of your home. Use rugs or carpeting where appropriate, but do not put them together in one room.

Make It Quiet

The smaller the space, the quieter you want it to be. If you're buying carpet, or even an area rug, be sure to get the best, thickest padding available.

Cork flooring is also a practical choice if you have high vaulted or cathedral ceilings that echo every sound. It's sound absorbent, stain resistant, and soft under foot.

Conversely, stone floors are elegant but can be very cold, noisy, and hard on your back, especially in the kitchen, so if you are sensitive to noise, consider this before you invest in one.

Make It Light

Your new home may get plenty of natural daylight, but you'll still need artificial light to enhance the space in the evening, when it's cloudy or raining, during the shorter days of winter, and, if you live in a colder climate, during those months when you're less likely to spend as much time outdoors. Light is even more important to us, psychologically, when we live in smaller spaces, as it may compensate somewhat for our limited square footage. So that they don't make you feel claustrophobic, small rooms need to be bright rooms. Make sure your entrance hall is light, bright, and welcoming when you walk in the door.

You will need both general and task lighting to provide not only more than one source of light but different levels for different purposes. And you may also choose to add accent lights to illuminate your artwork or plants.

Although some people are tempted to install skylights to maximize natural light, I don't generally recommend them because they often become damaged and leak, and they are very difficult to clean. There are, however, many other ways to bring more light into your life.

What about Bedrooms?

Yes, you need darkness to sleep, but what about all the daylight hours? To make your bedroom feel welcoming and cheerful when you're awake, be sure to have both general illumination and task lighting, as well as a window treatment that will allow in the maximum amount of daylight that is available. From a practical point of view, if you're dressing in there, it's a good idea to be able to see the colors of your clothing, but psychologically as well, you don't want to feel as if you're living in a cave.

You also need to be able to read in bed. Some people use both bedside table lamps and clip-on headboard lamps for reading, but that's aesthetically redundant. You should pick one type of lamp that provides all the illumination you need. My personal favorites are swing-arm lamps with three-way bulbs that are either hardwired inside the wall or have wires that are hidden by metal cord covers. Swing-arm lamps come in many sizes and styles, and with built-in dimmers. For maximum light, use linen or silk shades.

Conventional table lamps with three-way bulbs in metal or porcelain are another fine choice, so long as they are the right size, 22

Swing-arm lamps offer good, flexible lighting, both literally and figuratively.

to 28 inches high (and neither too small nor too large for your bedside table) and have translucent shades that allow light to filter through.

Be sure to center your bedside lamps on the tables, or have them swing above them, if they are hung on the wall.

A pair of lamps that provide a total of 300 watts will also serve as general illumination in a bedroom so that additional overhead lighting is not necessary. If you do require more light, a third lamp can be placed on a bureau to illuminate the other side of the room.

Mirrors, Glass, and Metal Create Space, Shine, and Light

If you have a window that gets good natural light, hanging or leaning a large framed mirror on the opposite wall will reflect the view and bring the light from outdoors to the opposite end of the room, creating the illusion that you have two windows and making the room seem bigger and brighter.

If you do not have space on the wall across from a window, try hanging a mirror on an adjacent wall that is at least 36 inches wide. This will give the impression that the window is bigger than it actually is.

In a long, narrow room, hang a large mirror on one of the long walls to make the room feel wider and more open. You can also hang a big, vertical mirror on a short wall at the end of a hallway to make the hall feel longer than it actually is.

Mirroring the back of a built-in and adding recessed lights will brighten the space at night and create a sense of additional depth by reflecting whatever is displayed on the shelves.

Have a glazier install mirror on any plain console or Parson's table,

A large mirror leaning against the wall doubles the light and view from a window on the opposite side of this room.

mirroring the entire piece, legs and all, to create an entirely new, glamorous look that will brighten your entire room.

If you already have a piece of mirrored furniture, such as a bureau, use it in the entrance foyer or a bedroom. Combined with wood furniture, it would be considered too feminine for the living room.

You can also mirror the narrow vertical sides of your window (called reveals) if you have a wonderful view that is not directly visible from every angle. One downsizing couple I worked with had a beautiful but indirect river view from two of the windows in their living room and one in the bedroom. I suggested that they mirror the sides of the reveals that face the water, and now they're delighted to be able to enjoy the view from their bed or when they're seated in living room instead of just when they're standing directly in front of the windows.

A glass-topped coffee table (with rounded corners or set in a wood frame), glass lamps, a glass vase, or even a collection of decorative glass balls, is not only translucent but also reflects light and makes any space seem more open, elegant, and airy.

By the same token, if you have a lot of wood pieces, adding brass, steel, or silver accents will create shine and make your room appear brighter.

General Lighting

General lighting usually means ceiling fixtures of some sort or uplit torchieres. While I like all sorts of floor lamps, torchieres are my least favorite option because they usually cast unattractive shadows on the ceiling and walls. If your ceilings are low, I recommend lighting that is flush with the ceiling, such as recessed or tiny halogen track spotlights, rather than something suspended like a chandelier.

Two types of lighting I never recommend are globe-like, half-bowl shaped, or flat hanging fixtures that light up the ceiling really well but cast unattractive shadows over the rest of the room. If you purchase a new lighting fixture, be sure that it harnesses the light and casts it downward so that your room and its furnishings are well lit.

Recessed halogen high hats—my favorites—provide full-spectrum lighting and taking up less room than larger floods. They can be used directly over conversation areas in family rooms and living rooms, in a row of three over the dining table, as well as in hallways and bathrooms. Adding one more hidden high hat in each corner of the room will give the space more evenly distributed ambient light. The actual sources of light are relatively hidden from view, which makes the space appear more open and airy than it would with conspicuous, suspended lighting fixtures. Be sure to get black baffles, which line the interior of the fixtures and cut the glare more effectively than chrome, white, or brass baffles, and therefore call less attention to the lighting.

If your new, smaller home has an open floor plan that combines two or three rooms without the separation of doors or archways, it is even more important not to have suspended ceiling fixtures.

One of my clients downsized to a house whose kitchen, dining room, and living room all open into one another. In the kitchen she had suspended a ceiling fan, over the dining table she'd hung a chandelier that she brought from her larger home, and in the living room she had centered over the coffee table another medium-sized lighting fixture that had been in her former family room. The minute anyone walked through the front door, the first thing they saw were all of the suspended fixtures, hung at different heights and competing for attention . . . total chaos.

Within two weeks of our meeting she removed the fixtures and had an electrician install recessed high hats throughout the space. She also changed the old white kitchen fan to a more modern steel model with a recessed halogen spotlight hidden inside it to light her kitchen island. All three rooms now have an open, airy look and much better lighting as well.

Track lighting, which is available in white or black and comes in either 4- or 8-foot lengths, is movable (which high hats are not) and less expensive than recessed lighting. The small halogen spots that clip onto the tracks are unobtrusive and can be directed anywhere in the room you choose. Since the track and fixtures hug the ceiling, they give the effect of more vertical space and, besides giving the room sufficient general illumination, allow you to subtly play up your artwork and plants without having an additional uplight fixture sitting on the floor.

Lutron dimmer switches provide flexibility if you want more or less light, plus they save energy. And, of course, always be sure that your outlets and switch plates blend in with your walls. Metal switch plates are easier to paint than plastic.

Lighting manufacturers around the globe are continually introducing innovative new products that are more energy efficient. Check with your local lighting store, home improvement retailer, or online resource to keep abreast of the latest fixtures and bulbs that can brighten your home, save you money, and protect the planet.

Task Lighting

In addition to general lighting, you'll also need task lighting for working, reading, knitting, or whatever else you need more direct light to accomplish. This usually means either standing lamps or table lamps in both the living room and the bedroom.

If you are using table lamps, the size of the space and the size of the table will determine the size of the lamp, but not the amount of light you need or are able to get out of it. I can't tell you how many times I've gone to a client's home and found 60-watt bulbs in three-way lamps that were capable of holding up to 150 watts. Imagine, instead of a pair of lamps providing 120 watts for an entire room—too little for most spaces—they could have 300 watts simply by changing the bulbs! And if you're buying new shades, remember that a light-colored silk or linen will let the most light shine through, while heavy paper, dark-colored, or metal shades will cut the available light.

Like everything electrical, lightbulbs are changing rapidly. With greater emphasis on energy efficiency, conservation-conscious consumers are demanding bulbs that will not harm the environment, are less costly to burn, and are easy on their eyes. Compact fluorescent lightbulbs that claim to last five to seven years cost only $6 to $8 per bulb. They use a lot less power than traditional incandescent bulbs and have a built-in transformer that adapts to most any lamp. And while you're being kind to the environment, you're also being kind to yourself because you have to change the bulb a lot less frequently! As for aesthetics, compact fluorescent bulbs provide a much whiter, cooler light than their incandescent counterparts. Therefore, when purchasing bulbs, keep in mind that the lower the Kelvin rating of a compact fluorescent bulb, the softer the light. If you are using the bulbs for your home, a compact fluorescent with a 2,700 Kelvin rating will provide you with a warmer white light than one with a cooler 4,100

Kelvin rating. In a residence, compact fluorescent lighting is more appropriate for rooms that have practical rather than mostly social functions. You can use these money-saving bulbs in kitchens, bathrooms, garages, and hallways and on patios since compact fluorescent lightbulbs do not give off heat and, therefore, do not attract bugs. Many older people who require bright reading light might opt for 5,000 Kelvin compact fluorescent bulbs that provide stronger, whiter light. Energy-saving LED (light-emitting diode) bulbs are another option now in development for residential use because of their low energy consumption. But if you are lighting your living room and dining room, and these rooms are used mostly for entertaining guests, stick with softer, incandescent lighting.

One of my barometers for gauging the comfort of a home is how many places there are to read comfortably. Count to see how many you have—ideally, there should be three or more—and please (as your mother probably told you) don't ruin your eyes. Make sure your

IF YOU REALLY WANT A CHANDELIER

- Make sure that your fixture harnesses the light and casts it downward to avoid shadows.
- Use frosted bulbs and fit them with clip-on shades.
- Adjust the chain or cord to accommodate the height of your ceiling. The standard height for a chandelier over a table is 30 to 34 inches. If the ceiling is higher than 8 feet, you can raise the chandelier 3 inches for every additional foot of ceiling.
- The smaller your space, the less ornate (and overpowering) your chandelier should be, and the diameter should always be smaller than that of your dining table.
- When hanging a chandelier in an entrance area, be sure there's enough room for the door to swing open without hitting the fixture.

This diminutive fixture found its new home in a smaller dining area.

lamps are right next to your sofa, chairs, or bed—not 5 feet away—so that you're getting the most out of the light you have.

Remember that if you flank a sofa with lamps, your room will not only look better and be more balanced aesthetically, but two people will be able to read comfortably at the same time, instead of having to take turns (which so many of my clients seem to do!).

Space Savers

- If space is at a premium, a double pharmacy floor lamp or a table model on a small table between two chairs will provide good light for two people to read comfortably together.
- Wall-mounted swing-arm lamps can be used at either end of a sofa or a daybed in a guest room or a family room as well as in the bedroom when surface space is limited. Remember to use bulbs with the highest wattage the lamps will allow.
- Sconces are now being made to hold bulbs of higher wattage, so if you're buying new ones, be sure they give off 100 to 150 watts. Otherwise, don't use them.
- This is key to remember in a limited space: If you don't have room for end tables, matching standing lamps at either end of the sofa will not only provide more general illumination and

If you use a couple of floor lamps as well as some other pairs, your room will be both well balanced and well lit.

reading light but will also add more cohesion because they are a balanced pair. And no, you don't need end tables at all if they don't provide storage and you have a good-size coffee table.

- If you have extremely limited space where even a small standard lamp shade on a standing lamp would take up too much room, you can use pharmacy lamps, which have small, unobtrusive metal shades.

- In a bedroom with limited space and a metal headboard, use small black or white metal clip-on lamps for reading.

The sconces lighting this dressing table are mounted directly on the mirror, making it appear as if the light itself is doubled.

- On a desk or a writing table with insufficient space for a table lamp, use a miniature halogen lamp.

- On the wall over a small dressing table, install two "movie star" makeup light strips that have several small round bulbs or one long vertical light on each side of the mirror. Alternatively, mount two sconces on the wall flanking a mirror or on the mirror itself, or buy a mirror that has built-in side lights. Taking the light off the table will conserve surface space.

- Install fluorescent strip lighting or "hockey puck" spots under kitchen cabinets to light up your counters.

- If there is shelving above a desk, use a clamp-on lamp attached to the bottom shelf to cast direct light onto the desk and save space.

Table lamps need to be in proportion to the size of the tables they stand on, and the shades need to be in proportion to the lamps. You don't want a big round lamp or a very tall one overpowering a small table. And a big, round shade that exceeds the diameter of a small table would be bumping into the wall. If you have lamps you think you can use, but your tables are smaller, try a small oval, rectangular, square, or pagoda-style shade, all of which take up less space than a round one.

If the bedside or end table is large, on the other hand, you don't want to pair it with a leggy candlestick lamp. You need something with more girth that will be more in proportion to the table. And remember always to place table lamps in the center of the table, not at the back, where they will look as if the wall is supporting them. Don't worry; it doesn't matter if the electric cord shows a bit on the top of the table.

Take Advantage of Your Height

It's possible that even though the rooms in your new home are smaller than those in your previous home, the ceilings will be higher. High ceilings make small rooms look larger, and you can take advantage of that height in a variety of ways. You can, of course, build in floor-to-ceiling bookcases with some closed storage (as long as you do not have vaulted ceilings!), but you can also use the space to hang art vertically instead of stretching it along the wall horizontally. If, for example, you have several pairs of artwork—a pair of botanicals, a pair of animal prints, etc.—you can hang up to four sets of uniformly framed pieces, one on top of the other. If the prints or drawings are of different sizes, you can hang them with the largest on the bottom and the small-

A vertical arrangement of art can complement a high ceiling.

Pairs of family photos in like frames can be hung vertically, and to make the display more dramatic, you could use white frames and paint the wall behind the photos a darker color.

est on top, so long as all the pieces are framed alike. Or, if you have a lot of artwork, you can cover an entire wall, virtually floor to ceiling, to create a dramatic effect. You can then also use a tall tree or an urn set on a pedestal and filled with tall branches on the other side of the room to balance the vertically hung artwork.

When they see high ceilings in their new home, many people are tempted to rush out and buy a tall ready-made piece of furniture to fill the space, but I don't necessarily recommend going in that direction, especially if you're not sure how long you will be staying in your home. The next place you move to may not have such high ceilings, which means that you'll no longer be able to use what you have. And if you do opt for an especially tall built-in, be sure to have the carpenter construct it in sections so that if you eventually move to a home with standard-height ceilings, you will be able to reconfigure the piece and continue to use it.

Fabrics That Flatter Smaller Spaces

The same thing I said about wallpaper and window coverings holds true for upholstery choices. Large, colorful, busy patterns can be overwhelming in a small room. A monochromatic color scheme and light, solid, neutral-colored fabrics will help the furniture appear to blend into the space, making the room look larger and feel airier, which will also leave you feeling more relaxed. Textured fabrics of all kinds add visual and tactile interest, yet keep the space feeling tranquil, especially if they conform to the room's color scheme.

If you do use patterns, choose something small and tidy like stripes, pin dots, small checks, or even harlequin prints and use a more colorful, assertive pattern as an accent on your throw pillows. Avoid using pattern on pattern for window treatments or upholstery because it can create visual overload in a small room.

Expand the Space You Have

As you did when you were looking for additional storage space, you need to look up, down, and around to find ways to expand the space you have by utilizing the areas you may have thought of as "dead space" or making others work in new ways.

I did this for a client who had moved from a house to a condo and no longer had a family room/den. She did, however, have a patio, which I suggested she enclose with screens and glass sliders. She then furnished it with rattan pieces she already owned, added durable tile flooring, and purchased a large teak table with a built-in lazy Susan and teak folding chairs that she could use both as a desk and for entertaining guests. Even though she didn't have any more actual space, she did now have an additional room.

Here are a couple of other ideas for creating usable rooms where you thought none existed.

- **Look under the stairs.** Certainly, this area can be used to build a storage closet, but if there is sufficient space, another option would be to create a small, cozy reading nook by moving in a comfortable chair, a good lamp, and a small table, and maybe even a low bookcase. If the niche has sufficient height, you might also consider placing a desk or a writing table and a chair in that area.

- **Co-opt your balcony.** Many newer condos and town houses have small balconies that add an architectural element but are not really intended as usable space—but they can be. You can buy a ready-made spiral staircase that is no more than 3 feet in diameter, add a banister, and, with the help of a contractor, turn your balcony into a home office, a library, or even a sleeping area for guests.

In a Smaller Space, Less *Truly* Is Best

The less you have on your surfaces, the roomier your home will appear. In fact, I generally advise clients to keep tables and windowsills clear of clutter no matter how large their home is. A few accessories go a long way, and collections of small objects or photographs in like framing materials can be effectively displayed on several narrow, wall-mounted, wooden shelves.

Another tidy way of displaying accessories without overwhelming a room is to place a small collection of like objects on a tray on your coffee table or a console. And, as an exception to my own rule, if you have a deep bay window and don't want or need to use it as a window seat, you can use it as a surface to display a large collection or a group of family photos (in like frames, of course). Remember to place the largest pieces or photos in the back, closest to the window, and graduate down to the smallest objects or pictures in the front row, where they are easy to see.

Keeping photos or collections together in one place makes the visual display more dramatic and less overpowering. You can display more than one collection in a single room, but they ought to be different from one another and kept in separate areas.

GOOD BUYS

FLOR offers stylish, affordable carpet and sisal tiles that are great for wall-to-wall "carpeting" or for creating a customized rug. Other advantages of this floor covering is that it does not require glue for installation and if one tile becomes very soiled it can be lifted up, washed, hosed down, or replaced immediately if you keep a spare stored in the closet. Plus, the tiles are easy to cut with an X-Acto knife, if necessary.

Curran FLOOR has a Swedish woven vinyl floor covering called Bolon that looks like a rug but is wipeable and easy to clean. This is terrific to use as a runner in an entrance hallway or as a rug in a covered patio area or childrens' room.

Displaying a collection on small, wall-mounted shelves keeps surfaces clear of clutter.

Use a tray to keep a small tabletop collection organized and tidy.

Gaiam is an eco-friendly company that offers, among other things, organic, mold-resistant plasters and pigments in several neutral colors that can be applied to walls to create a textured look.

Lee's Studio, Restoration Hardware, Williams-Sonoma, and Pottery Barn have a wide variety of modern and traditional table and floor lamps and shades in various sizes.

The Sharper Image carries a library lamp with a dimmer that allows you to adjust the light.

Lowe's and Home Depot have lamp departments that carry good, inexpensive basics and assorted shades.

The Noguchi Museum Store offers airy and simple but elegant paper "light sculptures" that provide soft illumination and work well over a dining table.

For an unobtrusive, almost flat track lighting system, check out the Kreon Prologe 80 In-Line system, which is made of aluminum and is designed for installation inside of ceilings made of drywall.

Restoration Hardware, Pottery Barn, and other sources also sell large lamp shades to hang over a dining table that harness the light down, look clean, and work with all design styles.

West Elm, among other companies, carries simple sheer nylon, silk, cotton-linen, or velvet ready-made curtains in a number of solid colors that will dress up a window without creating a heavy, bulky look.

For attractive wooden trays that can be used to display a collection, try Williams-Sonoma Home or Horchow.

7. Make It Multifunctional

WHEN YOU'RE MOVING to a smaller space, your rooms and your furniture may have to serve more than one purpose. Even if you're not living in a studio apartment, you may not have the luxury of designating one room for dining, another for sitting around or entertaining guests, and a third for work, letter writing, or paying bills. A guest room may be doubling as an office, a dining table may also do duty as a desk, and a sofa may be called into service for sleeping when you have overnight guests. The key to having all this work for you is to make your space and your furnishings as multifunctional as possible. We've already talked about pieces that double as storage—ottomans that open, trunks, chests, tables with doors or drawers, for example. But there are many more strategies for making what you have serve more than one purpose.

Finding a Place That Works for Work

Even before I learned that it's bad feng shui, I've always maintained that it's not a good idea for your bedroom to double as an office. When I first opened Use What You Have Interiors in 1981, I worked at a drop-leaf desk across from my bed. As a result, even when I sat propped up against my headboard reading at night, I would be constantly reminded of the work I had to do, and, of course, whenever the business telephone rang in the evening or on a weekend, it distracted me. After three months I knew it was time to relocate Use What You Have's "office" to my dining room.

Having a computer on the end table next to your bed, or your bills stacked on a writing table across the room, is not conducive to peaceful sleep. That said, however, if you have an extra bedroom you can make it serve more than one purpose.

Although a traditional pullout sofa is always an option, it might mean moving a lot of furniture when you need to open it. Another choice would be to use a cot-size daybed as a sofa by getting a fitted cover and arranging large, color-coordinated pillows against the wall. The cot is narrow enough to sit on comfortably and wide enough for a guest to sleep on. It will also take up less room than a pullout sofa not only because it doesn't need a lot of space in front of it but also because it is narrower and doesn't have arms! Call an upholsterer to create a tailored cover that will coordinate with your décor.

I did this for one of my Florida clients. We created a home office in her second bedroom, which included a daybed that her son can sleep on whenever he visits. She enjoys the daybed too because when he isn't there, she can stretch out on it and read. There's also a bureau in which she stores her paperwork, with a couple of empty drawers for her son's belongings. And the closet space is divided the same way.

As I suggested in Chapter 4, you can also flank a daybed with two-drawer wooden file cabinets with a pair of table lamps on top to serve as both night tables and office storage. The file cabinets come in a number of stains, and if you add a desk or even a writing table in the same or a similar finish plus a chair on wheels in a match-

A stylish daybed serves as a comfortable place to read and does double duty as a guest bed when needed.

ing or coordinating color, your guest room office will be virtually complete. One caveat: If you have a rolling desk chair, be sure you have a floor protector so that you don't destroy your carpet or wood floor.

To make the room even more versatile, hang a television on the wall or place it on a pedestal on the desk or a bureau and you've created an instant den that will also be appreciated by your guests, who may want to watch TV in their room.

If you do choose this option, look for an armchair-type desk chair that can be upholstered in a fabric to match or coordinate with the others in the room.

WORK OUT IN YOUR WORK ROOM

Your larger home might have had room for work-out equipment that simply won't fit in your new, smaller space. If that's the case, a folding treadmill that can be stored along with a few hand weights and a yoga mat in a closet will make the office/guest/TV room even more multifunctional.

If you have very little space, you might consider a Murphy bed or bunk beds that are attached to the wall and fold up flat when they're not being used. To use all of the space you have, if the bed isn't opened very often you can position either file cabinets on wheels or your desk and chair in front of it, either pushed right up against it or with a small space in between so that you can sit with your back to the bed, facing into the room. Another alternative is to place the desk perpendicular to the upright bed. Remember that you don't always have to place all your furniture against the walls.

If you do combine your guest room and home office, remember that your guests will need a place to put their clothing. If there isn't much drawer space, you can keep a folding luggage rack in a closet so that they'll be able to keep things right in the suitcase and still have it neat and accessible. Guests will also require both privacy and window coverings that keep the sun out while they're sleeping.

Yet another workspace option, if you don't have that extra bedroom, is to call the dining area into service between meals, as I did. You could, of course, simply work at the dining table, but if you don't need a large standard table all the time, you can opt for a drop-leaf table that stands against the wall with both leaves folded down when it's not in use for eating. Place a chair at either end and, when you need to work, flip up one leaf and pull a chair around and you have an instant desk. Keep a small file cabinet on wheels near the table and store folding chairs with slipcovers in a closet to use when you have guests.

Finally, you could have a desk and file drawers built into a niche, along a short wall, or on a window wall if there is one in the dining area. During the workday, the dining room table can then serve as an extra work surface, and when you "quit" for the day, the whole work space can be closed up and hidden from view.

By the way, if you have a baby, or a grandchild who will be spending the night, consider a crib with a drawer underneath that converts into a junior bed. Most children can use a junior bed until they start school, and the smaller sleeper takes up much less space than a conventional bed.

Also, if necessary, the top of a regular bureau can be used as a changing table with the addition of a special pad that is sold at most children's stores.

Create a Dual-Purpose Dining Table

A round pedestal table that raises and lowers by remote control can serve as a dining table during meals when it's in the "up" position and the chairs are pulled around it, and then lowered to serve as a coffee table when the chairs are moved away, thus transforming your dining room into a family room or a formal reception space with the push of a button. When I designed one for my New York home, my formal dining room, which had previously been the least used room, turned into a dining room/library/media room and became the most used space in our home.

Another option would be to do as one of my clients did. She didn't have a proper dining table, but she had a 48-inch-long by 30-inch-wide wooden coffee table in her living room. Although she wanted to have dinner parties, she didn't want to ask her friends either to eat with their plates on their laps or to sit on the floor around the coffee table, so we used what she had to solve her problem. A carpenter removed the existing wooden legs from the table and built two new matching sets of screw-on legs, one set at coffee table height (17 inches) and the other at dining height (29 inches). He also gave the tabletop several coats of polyurethane to protect it from spills, and now, by simply changing the legs, my client is able to serve dinners for four.

If you like to eat in front of the television, alone or with a friend, consider buying Brookstone's small coffee table with storage that can be raised from coffee table to dining height (see "Good Buys").

Sleeping in the Living Room?

Although having rolled-up Japanese futons on hand for overnight guests is always an option, they can be a bit bulky if you are short of closet space. And there are even greater spatial challenges if you use your living room for sleeping every night. When one of my clients decided it was time to simplify his life, he moved from a classic, postmodern one-bedroom apartment to a much smaller one-bedroom in a landmarked building. Not only were the living room and bedroom much smaller, but he'd decided to use the tiny bedroom as his office. That meant he would essentially be living in a studio, and he needed to figure out where he was going to sleep.

He certainly could have chosen a convertible sofa or a daybed that would double as a couch, but he already had a modern sofa upholstered in navy velvet that he really liked and wanted to keep. In the end, I suggested that he buy a Murphy bed. The one he selected is made of white wood and has built-in closed storage on either side. When it's closed, it virtually "disappears into the woodwork," and when it's open, there's a lovely photograph of a Buddhist monk hanging above the bed and two small reading lights, in addition to built-in halogen spots above the headboard. His new room is now completely multifunctional, and no one would ever know there was a bed hiding in the wall. In addition, his home office space is separated from his living and sleeping space, which makes his downtime more restful.

Despite all the jokes and sitcom-type scenarios of people getting trapped, Murphy beds are extremely practical, are more comfortable than most sleep sofas, provide storage space, and come in so many sizes, styles, and finishes that there's sure to be one appropriate for virtually any home.

Screen It Off!

In Chapter 2, I talked about the possibility of using bookcases as room dividers, but there are also times when you might want a divider that's more flexible. For example, you might have designated a corner of your living room as office space that you don't want to look at when it's not in use. (As in a bedroom, a blinking computer in the living room may make it harder for you to declare the workday over and relax.) Movable dividers are becoming more available and much easier to use. Decorative screens come in a number of styles, sizes, and finishes. Some have canvas pockets and others multiple picture frames so that they not only define and divide the space but also serve as a vertical decorative accent.

GOOD BUYS

Oriental Furniture has lots of great-looking screens in many styles and finishes at very affordable prices that can be used as room dividers or even as a headboard for your bed.

Design Within Reach has an accordion-pleated "textile softwall" that is 6 feet high and can be extended to 20 feet long. It is the ultimate portable wall as it is made of an indestructible Dupont fiber-based sheet material. It is meant to be arranged in soft curves, and is also easily retractable.

Restoration Hardware offers a linen fabric Memo Screen with criss-crossing ribbons into which you can tuck photographs and that can also be used as a headboard.

Art-Is-Life and Bill Russell Studio both offer dozens of dividers that can also be used as decorative wall accents.

dVider offers affordable, easy to assemble and disassemble, 4- or 6-foot-wide space dividers either in solid cotton sail or custom printed. They come in one- to four-sail configurations.

Levenger offers office furniture that looks as if it belongs in the living room.

Pier 1 and Loft 21 (divisions of the same company) offer a convertible desk. It has four drawers and a panel that pulls out to create a comfortable kneehole opening for legs. When the panel is in the closed position the desk looks just like a chest of drawers.

The Company Store sells a unique, three-in-one piece of furniture in mission style that starts as a console with two drawers and would make a great hall piece. The 40 × 20-inch console opens into a 40 × 40-inch gaming or dining table that seats four and to which you can add two leaves to make a 40 × 72-inch dining table that seats six. There are also folding chairs to match the table that can be purchased in sets of two.

Pottery Barn carries a few small, off-white bedside tables with storage for reading material.

The Amelia magazine storage table from A Touch of Class has a closed storage compartment, a side magazine rack, and a pull-out tray. It comes in off-white and is small enough to fit in a tiny bedroom or alongside a sleep sofa in an office/guest room.

Brookstone makes an affordable foldaway treadmill on wheels that is easy to use, and The Sharper Image sells an inexpensive elliptical strider that can be stored under a bed.

Brookstone also carries a coffee table that comes in several finishes and converts to a dining-height table.

Target's convertible coffee table, called the Esprit, has an egg-shaped metal base that gives it a modern look. It raises from $12^{1}/_{2}$ to $32^{1}/_{2}$ inches and can seat four for dinner.

Another source for an up-and-down table is Jensen-Lewis in New York City. Go to their Web site to see what it looks like.

For information about tables that go up and down by remote control, contact redecorate.com.

Design Within Reach has a "sliding" sofa with a back panel that drops down to make a full- or queen-size bed and a handy "bingo pouf" that opens to a full-length sleeper and, when closed, is extremely compact and serves as a stool or a side table (with the addition of its own bent maple tray attached to the top).

Resource Furniture sells wall-mounted bunk beds that fold down flat against the wall, unlike a Murphy bed.

For trundle beds, try Charles Rogers.

For Murphy beds, check with Murphy Bed Company, Murphy Wall-Beds Hardware, or your local Murphy bed store.

8. For Kitchens and Bathrooms Only

F YOUR PREVIOUS HOME had a spacious eat-in kitchen or a bathroom the size of one at the Ritz, these may be two rooms where you feel particularly spatially challenged. They are also the two places where organization and proper storage can make the difference between serenity and insanity when you're trying to prepare a meal or relax in a hot bath after a long, stressful day. And finally, they're two rooms where safety is important.

Hints and Tips for Kitchen and Bathroom Safety

- The handles on drawers and cabinets should be easy to grasp with wet hands and should have rounded rather than sharp, pointy edges.
- On room doors, lever handles are easier to grasp than knobs.
- If you're replacing floors, think nonshiny (which means nonslippery) and not so porous that they impede easy movement.
- Be sure to install angled grab bars in every bathroom shower and above every tub to prevent dangerous slips.
- Have anti-scald devices installed in showers.
- In bathrooms, use only mats that have nonskid or rubber backing.
- If possible avoid countertops with pointy corners.
- Keep small appliances unplugged when not in use.
- Purchase a small rubber mat for the floor in front of your kitchen sink to catch drips that might make a floor slippery.
- If possible, store heavy pots and pans in drawers that are easy to open so that you don't strain your back or shoulder. Otherwise, keep them within easy reach on a wall or a hanging rack.
- Use stools with back support.
- If you're creating a center island or positioning a small table, be sure to leave enough room so that you can open the oven door while standing in front of it. Working from the side leads to arm burns.

Get Cooking in a Smaller Kitchen

If there's one place where storage really matters it's the kitchen—because everyone has so much stuff! Dishes, glasses, pots and pans, cutlery, utensils, not to mention the food itself, all need to be stored and accessed easily on a regular basis.

I hope you've taken the advice offered in Chapter 2 and weeded out all the small appliances and gadgets you haven't used in years (like the meat grinder handed down by your grandmother) as well as all the stuff you didn't actually discard when you "replaced" it. And that you've assessed what may need to be spruced up or replaced. I'm certainly not suggesting that you gut the kitchen and start over, or even that you replace the appliances, so long as they work and look good. But kitchens can appear dated very quickly, and sometimes a few simple changes can create a whole new look. If you do buy new appliances, choose smaller, slimmer models that will save you both space and money. Narrower stoves and refrigerators will allow you to fit in more cabinets and countertops. In addition, a pull-out-drawer-style dishwasher will take up less space and hold just as many dishes. And keep in mind that, as a general rule, whatever investment you put into upgrading your kitchen will be returned 100 percent if you decide to sell.

If you are making changes, keep in mind that a "busy" patterned countertop will make the space look smaller while one that is more neutral will make it appear larger. White appliances look best with white cabinets. With wood cabinets, use stainless steel or black appliances and avoid white ones if you possibly can.

When clients are lucky enough to have one or more windows in their kitchen, I give them the same kind of advice about curtains that I do about rugs in the dining room: *Don't use them.* Kitchen curtains are notorious grease-grabbers, so if you think you *must* cover your windows, use a pleated Duette shade that can be pulled all the way up while you're cooking.

Modernize the Cabinets

Built-in cabinets are costly to replace, but resurfacing or replacing the doors or even just the decorative hardware can give them an entirely different look at a fraction of the cost.

Hardware generally comes in standard sizes and has either one or two screws holding it in place. If you unscrew one of the handles you have, you can take it with you when you shop to be sure what you're buying to replace it will fit. When you're choosing, style is, of course, a consideration, but also consider how easy the handles are to grasp and look for those that are rounded, not sharp and pointy.

My cousins moved from a home in Rhode Island to a condo in Laguna Woods, California, where they have much less square footage. Among several things they did to spruce up their new, smaller home was to have the kitchen cabinets professionally relacquered and all the hinges and hardware replaced. The insides of the cabinets were repainted with white semigloss, and they purchased white vinyl tiles on sale for a dollar each and used them to line the bottom of every shelf. (They did this themselves using an X-Acto knife.) The new, smooth tile surface is not only attractive but also makes it easy to slide the contents in and out. Now it looks as if they have brand-new cabinets.

An even less expensive option, if one or two of the cabinet doors is damaged, would be to remove the door entirely and use the open shelves for dishes or glassware you use frequently and want to be easily accessible. Just remember that if you do this, you'll need to keep the contents neat and tidy 24/7. For that very reason, I don't recommend storing pantry items on open shelves. If your new kitchen has an open-shelf pantry, you can simply hang a curtain or have doors made to keep the contents out of sight.

If you are replacing the entire cabinet, either because your cabinets are damaged or because you want a different style, be sure that you choose new base cabinets with full-extension drawers that make it much easier to see what is in the back and access what you've got.

Keep It Classic, Keep It Neutral

If you're painting or updating the kitchen, you may be tempted by a patterned wallpaper or a bright color, but I strongly advise against these options for both kitchens and bathrooms. For one thing, a color that's trendy today may well be dated in a year or two. Or the pattern or color that's calling out to you now may quickly lose its siren-like appeal. If you're considering resale, you need to consider that your favorite color may not be so inviting to buyers. But even if you think you'll be staying forever, if your home has an open plan and you paint the kitchen green to match your living room color scheme, what will happen if you decide to redo the whole living room in shades of blue two years from now? White, ecru, and linen are classic, easy to clean, and timeless;

work with everything; and make any space look bigger, brighter, and fresher—all important considerations when you are downsizing.

There are dozens of "whites" to choose from, as well as many other neutral shades, from light cream to deep mocha, that are easy to live with and will not inhibit resale. If you're still craving a bright or strong color, you can satisfy your cravings with accessories—dish towels, pot holders, place mats, and even canisters, all of which are inexpensive and easy to replace. If there is space on one wall, you can also hang a piece of "food-themed" artwork that incorporates your favorite colors.

Upgrade the Sink

Like the hardware on your cabinet doors, the faucet on your sink is probably a standard size. Does it have a spray attachment and a goose-neck faucet that allows you to get that soup or pasta pot underneath it?

Is there a soap dispenser so that you can clear the counter of that unsightly bottle of dishwashing liquid? If not, and if the faucet is stainless steel, you may be able to retro-fit the sink with these useful amenities. Or you can simply replace the whole faucet set at substantially less cost than replacing the entire sink.

A gooseneck faucet with a built-in sprayer is handy and saves space. Be sure to install a soap dispenser, too.

Maximize Your Surface Space

In smaller kitchens, surface space is always at a premium. As a general rule, it's therefore wise to keep what space you have as free of clutter as possible. Not only will you have more room to work and cook but also the space will feel better visually. Microwaves, toaster ovens, grids to hang stemware, paper towel holders, even cookbook holders and knife holders (I love the black and aluminum models that coordinate with the black and stainless accents in most kitchens) can be installed under the cabinets instead of standing on the counter. Spice shelves can be hung on the wall, and a number of spice racks are also made to fit inside small drawers. Small appliances you use frequently can be neatly displayed on a wall shelf to get them off the countertop, and those you do not use daily, such as a blender or a food processor, can be stored in cabinets.

For additional workspace, consider a drop-down shelf attached to the wall that can be opened up for use when you need it. If you have very limited space, have the shelf made in a half-round shape. If you have more room or a long, narrow kitchen, the drop leaf can be a longer rectangle with rounded corners.

If you're lucky enough to have room for a small center island, you can have one made without spending a lot of money by installing a base cabinet in the middle of the kitchen and adding a top made of Corian, mica, or granite. Just be sure the top has a small overhang all around, with one or two sides deep enough for two or three people to sit on stools with their knees comfortably underneath and for the stools to be pushed in when they're not in use (so that they don't obstruct the traffic pattern). Have the corners of the island top rounded to make it safer to walk around and leave at least 30 to 36 inches of open space surrounding the island for a comfortable traffic pattern. The base unit

Even a small center island provides additional space for food prep, storage, and even informal dining.

will also provide a drawer for silverware or utensils, plus extra closed storage space on the bottom that's easy to reach.

More Space-Savers

- A collapsible chrome cart can function as an island and a server and can be folded flat and stored in a closet when it's not in use.
- Hang a pot rack on a wall or from the ceiling—over a center island or over the window. Some even come with lights to augment your task lighting. Hang a plate rack above the sink. That way you can wash your plates and put them right on the rack and any water will drip back into the sink. Some plate racks also come with a shelf or hooks to hold cups.
- Hang racks for holding plastic wrap, aluminum foil, and garbage bags on the inside of the cabinet doors under the sink.
- Attach corkboard or cork tiles to the inside of a cabinet door to create a "message center" that doesn't take up precious wall space.
- To maximize storage space, purchase a rack to hold pot lids that fits on the inside of the cabinet door.
- Fit the inside of your cabinets with rubber-covered wire or metal racks that allow you to use the whole space without stacking dif-

Hang your lids over the pot handles to keep them together and save space.

ferent size dishes on top of one another. Larger cabinets can also be fitted with lazy Susans that bring what you're looking for right to your fingertips. The same idea applies to those condiment shelves in your fridge that seem to swallow up jars of mustard and jams.

- If there's room between the tops of your cabinets and the ceiling, you may be able to add a track and small sliding doors that match your cabinets or wall color and will allow you to store items you don't use very often out of sight and also free of kitchen grease.

- If you purchase a new washer and dryer, consider buying machines that have storage pedestals underneath to house laundry supplies. Raised, front-loading machines will also make loading the wash easier on your back.

- If there is a narrow open space between a wall and your cabinets, have a carpenter hang a door to enclose the entire niche. Use the space to store your broom, Swiffer, mop, or extra paper goods or shopping bags. The door front can match either the cabinets or your wall color.

- If you have attractive copper pans or even molds that you actually use, consider hanging them on the wall as decoration. They will be attractive to look at and easier to access.

- If you don't plan to do a lot of cooking (many downsizers are empty nesters and have determined that their days of elaborate dinner parties are over) you can purchase a combination microwave and convection oven, do away with your conventional oven entirely, and use the space under the stovetop for additional closed storage.

- To maximize counter space, instead of a permanent dish drainer, get a collapsible one that can be folded and stored under the sink when it's not in use.

Make the Most of Your Bathrooms

As a general rule, smaller homes mean smaller (and fewer) bathrooms, so you'll really need to make the most of what you've got. We tend to keep a lot of "stuff" in our bathrooms, from toiletries to medications to linens and towels. Sometimes it can seem almost impossible to figure out where to put it all and maintain a sense of order and serenity.

If you have only one bathroom, you'll certainly want to keep it ready to receive guests. If there's more than one person using it, the problem may be compounded. There are, however, many simple strategies for making the most of the one you have.

Whenever Possible, Store It Out of Sight

As with every other room in your home, the more you are able to keep in drawers or behind closed doors, the more elegant and serene your bathroom will be.

- If the sink is attached to the wall and not enclosed and there's enough room, have it fitted with a vanity for storage. Or you can replace a small pedestal sink with an under-mounted or drop-in sink in order to get a bigger vanity with more storage. If you do opt for the larger vanity, consider a small round or oval stainless steel sink that will be both stylish and easy to clean. A vessel-style sink that sits on top of the counter rather than being recessed will allow for more storage inside the vanity, too.

A vessel-style sink is one way to maximize the storage space in the vanity underneath.

- If there's room above the toilet, hang a closed cabinet or a second, sleek, flat, mirrored medicine chest either sunk into or on the wall.

- If the existing mirrored medicine chest is showing its age, attach a wooden frame to cover the edges, which tend to show the most wear and tear. This will give the unit a more elegant look. The frames are available at Lowe's and Home Depot.

- If the only place for storage is over the sink, and if space allows, consider replacing the existing medicine chest with a larger one.

- If there is floor space between the sink and the toilet or elsewhere in the room, consider purchasing a chrome bathroom trolley (on wheels) to hold your cosmetics and hairstyling accessories. Or consider Pottery Barn's moisture-resistant, white wood Hotel Sundry Tower. The unit doesn't take up a lot of floor space but has four drawers and a small pullout shelf and would work equally well in a small kitchen.

NOWHERE TO HANG YOUR MEDICINE CHEST?

One of my clients had a big wall-to-wall mirror over the double vanity sink in her master bathroom. Since the mirror was hung on an exterior wall there was not enough depth to install a medicine chest. Instead, the client had hung the medicine chest on the small wall adjacent to the big mirror, where it looked out of place.

To correct the problem, we found an inconspicuous wall behind the bathroom door that backed onto the master bedroom closet. Not only was the wall deep enough to handle the medicine chest, but the chest itself was less obtrusive hidden behind the door.

Many homes have this same bathroom configuration. If yours does, too, look for a similarly hidden or unobtrusive spot to install your medicine cabinet.

Make It Look Bigger

If the tub isn't already enclosed, replacing the shower curtain with sliding clear glass, trackless doors will make the entire room seem larger because you'll be able to see all the way to the wall. Keep in mind that many bathrooms have a window in the tub area and a shower curtain not only cuts off 25 to 30 percent of the room but also blocks the light that comes from the window.

Clear glass shower and tub enclosures allow you to see the far wall, which makes the entire bathroom look bigger.

What you won't be able to do, however, is hide things behind the curtain. Buy a chrome caddy that fits right over the showerhead to hold soaps and shampoos and keep them off the rim of the tub where they make the room feel messy and cluttered. Or, if your bathroom has a windowsill inside the tub area that is deep enough to hold your hair products, get a chrome tray or basket to keep everything neatly in place.

SOFTEN IT UP

Although I've said it's best to keep the bathroom as uncluttered as possible, I do believe that it's nice to bring in one or two items to balance all those hard surfaces. A small orchid plant, an appropriate piece of artwork, a couple of pieces of sterling, or a small tray with perfumes are all touches that will soften and beautify the room without taking up too much space.

Small Bathroom Strategies

■ No linen closet? Besides storing linens in other places in your home, you can keep several neatly folded towels on a chrome shelf mounted on the bathroom wall. Many models even come with a bar underneath for hanging the towels that are in use. Yet another option would be a vanity that has open center

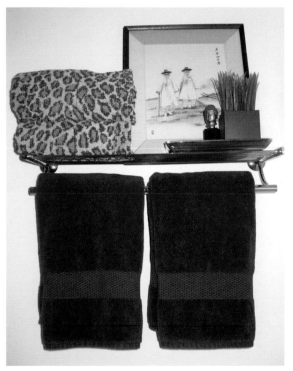

A chrome shelf unit with a towel bar below provides additional storage.

Accessories dress up this bathroom vanity. When the door broke and could not be repaired, one side of the large medicine chest became a display cabinet for perfume bottles and silver-framed photos.

A vanity with open shelves can be used to hold towels.

shelves on which you can keep a few neatly folded. If you are storing towels in plain sight, get a "decorator" look by first folding them in thirds lengthwise and then in thirds crosswise. You'll wind up with a nice, rounded shape that can be shelved end-out and look neat and attractive.

- No place to store extra toilet tissue? Unwrap a few rolls and keep them in a lacquered rattan basket right in plain sight and easy to access.

- Using grout the same color as your tiles will make the space look more expansive (and the same, of course, holds true for kitchens).

GOOD BUYS

The Kitchen

Williams-Sonoma, MetroKitchen, kitchensource.com, potracks. com, RangeCraft, Urban Archaeology, and PotRacksGalore all offer a variety of hanging pot racks (also known as enclumes).

Dom New York and Sirius both offer ceiling-mounted range hoods with lights that can be hung above an island cooktop.

To update countertops, backsplashes, and floors, try "slipcovers" made of stone or glass tiles from Granite Transformations that can be used to cover the existing surfaces.

To save counter space, get the Tools Design aluminum knife stand sold at the Museum of Modern Art in New York.

Lillian Vernon offers an under-cabinet kitchen organizer that keeps spices or vitamin bottles hidden when not in use.

Crate and Barrel, the Container Store, and Stacks and Stacks carry spice racks that fit inside of drawers.

The Elfa door and wall rack system, available at The Container Store and Organize.com, is a wire unit with adjustable shelving that can be mounted inside a solid or hollow door. Baskets to fit the shelves are available in three sizes.

Crate and Barrel's Somerset Kitchen Island is made of white wood, mounted on wheels, and includes three drawers, a two-door cabinet underneath, a towel rack, and a butcher-block top.

Improvements carries a folding chrome serving cart.

Design Within Reach, Williams-Sonoma Home, and All Barstools carry stylish counter stools.

Restoration Hardware carries good-looking storage pieces and small cabinets for the kitchen.

The Bathroom

Brookstone (for shower caddies)

Bowl and Board (for bath accessories)

Organize-It (for a variety of bathroom organizers)

Pottery Barn offers a really clever stainless-steel magazine rack to hang on the bathroom wall that has holders for two roles of toilet paper underneath.

Stacks and Stacks carries an inexpensive chrome unit with a hamper on the bottom, a center towel rack, and a top shelf that attaches to the back of the bathroom door and disappears from view when the door is open.

In addition to the Sundry Tower, Pottery Barn's Hotel Collection also includes a white wood ledge with five chrome hooks that's good for hanging towels and a robe and displaying perfume bottles.

Home Depot, Lowes, and other home improvement centers as well as Internet sellers offer ready-made wooden frames to fit standard medicine cabinet mirrors.

If you *must* have a shower curtain, Solutions offers one that cleverly includes two built-in towel bars so that the towels you are using hang in front of the curtain.

9. New Tactics for Living Smaller

OVING TO a smaller space will no doubt require some rethinking not only about your home's style and function but also about how you live your daily life. I suspect that at least some of you may be downsizing because you have reached the point where you want to find ways to simplify your life as much as possible, but some of you may also be collectors or pack rats. Whether you're a minimalist or a clutterer by nature, there are strategies you can use to make your move easier both mentally and physically.

When You Send Out
Moving Cards . . .

Collectors collect, and not only that, but their friends are constantly giving them gifts to add to their collection. If you're downsizing, you'll have to stop this madness, or at least stanch the flow. One client, whose well-meaning friends and relatives were constantly finding items to add to her turtle collection, found a solution—when she sent out moving cards, she added a line, worded to be light and amusing, asking these well-meaning people to please stop giving her turtles.

Keep It Clean
and Cohesive

When I say "clean" I don't mean just dusting and polishing—although that's important, too. I mean aiming for clean lines, uncluttered surfaces, and rooms that are neat and coordinated as well as comfortable. Basic strategies that hold for any home are all the more important when you move to a smaller space.

- Try not to mix different, contrasting shades of wood in the same room. Combining woods of different colors will make your space look more chopped up (and, therefore, smaller). Instead, use woods that are all of one shade—light, medium, or dark—but different types. For example, use a combination of bleached pine, light maple, and limed oak to give your room a more open, cohesive look.

- Keep all photographs and/or artwork framed in like materials and grouped together. Determine which framing material the majority of your photos are already in and change the rest to the same finish so that the whole grouping has a more pulled together look. The same rule applies to plant containers. Use all brass or steel, all clay or all black. Pick one finish and group all your plants together in one sunny corner to create a unified mini-garden.

A group of photographs, even though they are different sizes, can be matted and framed to create a grand, cohesive display.

Tall branches in a vase or an urn can be used to balance the height of a high piece of furniture on the opposite side of the room or to fill space in a room with high ceilings.

SMALL SPACE, NO CARE "PLANTS"

If you don't have room for plants in your new, smaller home or the inclination to care for them, find a corner for a small, 42-inch-high pedestal to hold an urn filled with tall willow branches, which are available at most florist shops and require no care and no watering. Just arrange them and let them dry naturally. This great alternative to a tree is dramatic, elegant, and carefree, and takes up almost no room. It's also the perfect solution to balancing a tall piece of furniture such as an entertainment unit or a high bookcase on the opposite side of the room. If you don't have a tall piece, hang artwork vertically on the opposite wall to balance the height of the branches.

ROTATE YOUR DISPLAYS

Photos in easel-back frames, collections, and even artwork on shelves will allow you to rotate your displays seasonally or just according to your mood. Having this flexibility is all the more important in smaller spaces, where you may not have the room to "show off" everything you have all at once. In addition to being practical, however, it's also fun to switch your accessories to reflect seasonal changes or to create holiday-themed displays.

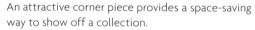

An attractive corner piece provides a space-saving way to show off a collection.

Use a large, colorful platter to rotate and display natural, seasonal objects.

- Whenever possible, hang TVs on the wall to maximize space. Keep the scale of the television in proportion to the size of your space. For a smallish room (under 14 feet long) a 30-to 40-inch screen would be a good size.

- Hang narrow wooden display shelves on the wall to show off framed photographs or collections, or hang the collection itself on the wall, rather than cluttering table surfaces.

- A small wooden corner unit won't take up a lot of space but can be used to show off a collection or family photos.

- Create as much balance and cohesion as possible by maximizing your use of pairs—lamps, end tables, chairs, prints, urns, and throw pillows. A corollary to Imelda's rule is that you can never have too many pairs!
- To make the room look bigger and feel more serene, leave one wall blank— that is, with absolutely nothing hung on it. Every room needs a place for our eyes to rest.

Here, a flat-panel television on a pedestal competes for attention with two pieces of art, each of which deserved its own space.

Without any distractions, the television wall looks less chaotic.

Develop New Habits

Little things mean a lot, and that's particularly true when space is limited. Some of you may always have been neat freaks, but for those of you who tend to let things pile up, it's time to change those "mañana" habits.

- Have a DustBuster or other handheld vacuum handy to keep your space clean and neat at all times.
- Be disciplined and hang up your clothing as soon as you take it off. Make your bed as soon as you get up. The less space you have, the more important it is to keep things neat and tidy.
- Put away dry cleaning in the closet immediately; don't let it hang around in a doorway because you're going to be wearing it soon anyway.
- Fold your laundry and put it away as soon as it comes out of the dryer. No carts full of clean laundry stashed behind the bedroom door, please.
- Give away, donate, or regift any gifts you're not going to use. Do it right away. Don't stash the item thinking that you'll do it next Christmas because by then you'll have forgotten all about it.
- Sort through and dispose of the junk mail you do receive every day. Not only will this help to keep surfaces clear of clutter, but you'll be a lot a less likely to lose a bill or some other important piece of mail.
- Throw away the newspaper every day, even if you haven't had time to read it. There's going to be more news—and another paper—tomorrow, and old news, after all, is no longer news.

- Cut down on your magazine subscriptions. Unread magazines can pile up before you know it, and, like newspapers, they just keep on coming. As soon as you receive a new issue, toss the old one. If you haven't read it all yet, chances are you never will!

USE YOUR COMPUTER TO END PAPER CLUTTER

nstead of storing boxes and boxes of paper records, you can keep your life—and your house—in order with a fast, inexpensive scanner that will transfer all that paper into digital files that are also easier to access when you need them. Just remember to back up your files!

Edit Your Clothing

Before you moved you weeded through all the clothing that had been hanging around and never leaving its hangers, so don't start collecting again. Use the "one in, one out" rule of thumb: If you buy something new, it has to replace something you no longer wear or need. Consider this a positive approach for shopaholics: If you delete, you can shop! One great way to recycle your clothing is to give things to a resale shop at the end of each season. That way, you'll not only make more room in your closet, you'll also have extra cash to buy something new.

Clean and store your clothes seasonally. Most dry cleaners offer storage that will get your out-of-season clothing out of your closet and into theirs. Weed it out before you clean and store it. If you haven't worn it all winter, you probably won't wear it next winter either, so why pay for the cleaning and storing?

Give Up Your Membership in the Price Club

Buying cartons of toilet tissue and paper towels, detergent by the gallon, and prepacked steaks by the dozens may have been a good idea when you had a basement and a giant freezer. You may have to start thinking smaller and shopping more often, but you probably won't need as much stuff anyway now that you are simplifying your life.

Remember to Plan for Your Pets

Your dog or cat may not care how your new home looks, but he or she will probably be a bit unsettled in a new and unfamiliar permanent home. If it is physically possible, take your pet to your new home before your actual move so that he can sniff around and get acquainted with the space. Take along a few toys for her to play with and leave them there so that the new space has your best friend's scent when he or she moves in.

Most dogs prefer to sleep under a piece of furniture, so factor this in when you're planning your new furniture arrangement. If you're not taking the baby grand piano, the dining table or any open, leggy piece of furniture might provide the perfect "canopy" for his bed. Also, a soft, round, cushion-style pet bed that can be squeezed into a smaller space is more adaptable than a hard, rigid one.

Kitty will probably find her own favorite spots to snooze, but finding the best place for her litter box is something to consider in advance, especially if you previously had three bathrooms and will now have only one. If you have a covered litter box, consider putting a basket of scented soaps on top to make this small space smell better.

GOOD BUYS

Pottery Barn's Olivia wall shelves, which can hold photos or collectibles, are available in white wood or mahogany stain. They're 8 inches deep and come in 24- to 36-inch lengths.

Home Decorators offers a wide assortment of affordable pedestals in wood, marble, or metal.

Orvis offers doggy beds in various fabrics and sizes, and they'll even monogram them for your pet.

If you want to hide your dog's bed, FunStuffForDogs.com makes a pet Murphy bed that takes up 10 inches of space and holds up to a 200-pound dog! It comes in three wood finishes.

Love That Cat carries wooden litter boxes in a choice of styles and stains, and most pet shops have attractive wicker covers that are big enough for even large cats.

One Year Later—
Time to Reassess

ONCE YOU'VE BEEN in your new home for a year, you probably have a good idea of what's working and what isn't. Maybe everything's perfect, and that's great, or maybe you got everything unpacked but never got around to "fine-tuning." Chances are that at least a few of your initial decisions could use a bit of tweaking. If so, it's time to ask yourself a few questions:

When I come home and open my front, door do I feel happy?

Do I have a place to hang visitor' coats (and my own)?

Will I be staying here longer than I originally expected?

Is there anything I wish I had that I don't?

Would I like a permanent place to keep my laptop set up?

Am I comfortable entertaining here?

Do I have enough comfortable seating for reading and for guests?

Can I get rid of old camera equipment that's taking up space, since my photos are now all digital?

Could I be using my kitchen workspace and storage space more efficiently?

Are there things up high that I'd like to have lower and more accessible?

Are there things I kept that I'm no longer using or have never used since I downsized?

Do I need better task lighting in the living room, home office, bathroom, or kitchen?

Have I used all of my closet space effectively?

Is it time to replace that rug I brought with me that doesn't really work with the new sofa?

Do I have enough space for overnight guests?

Is there a niche someplace where I could create more storage space?

Are there any other improvements I could make to increase my own comfort and add to the aesthetic value and equity of my home?

Generally speaking, the same rule of thumb holds true for your stuff as it does for your clothing: If you haven't used it, missed it, or remembered it in a year, you probably never will. If you moved things because you weren't sure whether or not you'd need or use them, and if you haven't needed or used them yet, it's time for them to go.

The same holds true for the furniture and accessories you put in storage "just in case" or because you "couldn't bear" to part with them. If "just in case" hasn't happened yet, it probably won't, and you've had a year to get used to living without them.

Now is also the time to revisit and reassess your off-site storage.

Look at the pictures you took. Is there anything in storage you could use to replace something you have? If so, go retrieve it.

Are there pieces you now know you'll never use again? If so, get rid of them and see if you can transfer what remains to a smaller storage unit that will cost you less each month. Did you stash things in cartons because you couldn't deal with ditching them? If so, go take a look; it might be time to say *arrivederci*. I know this sounds like a job

OUT WITH THE OLD, IN WITH THE NEW—TAX RECORDS

If you moved with the legally necessary seven years of tax records, now's the time to put in the new year's information and toss the one that's out of date. Use the same "one in, one out" rule you do for buying new clothes.

you would rather put off, but the sooner you do it, the more money you'll have to use for fun stuff. That alone ought to be a great reason to cut the cord and give up the storage unit.

Your goal over the last twelve months was to simplify your home and, therefore, your life. You've kept the best of what you had and rid yourself of clutter. When you look around, you're feeling good about your new home and all that you have accomplished. So, having reached this point, make a pledge to yourself that you won't reaccumulate all the "stuff" you were so glad to get rid of just a year ago. By consciously choosing to live with less you will continue to reap the rewards of having a simplified life: You'll have more time to relax and enjoy each day in your new, downsized home.

Sources

This information is accurate to the best of the author's knowledge as of the date of publication.

ABC Carpet and Home
    abchome.com
    212-472-3000
    Collapsible dining table

All Barstools
    allbarstools.com
    800-630-6105
    Counter stools

Alsto's
    alsto.com
    800-447-0048
    Nesting tables, bed risers

Art-Is-Life
    art-is-life.com
    Room dividers

Attic Dek
    atticdek.com
    Plastic storage racks

Bill Russell Studio
    billrussellstudio.com
    215-203-0068
    Room dividers

Bowl and Board
    bowlandboard.com
    617-661-0530
    Bath accessories

Brookstone
    Brookstone.com
    800-926-7000
    Foldaway treadmill,
    convertible coffee table,
    shower caddy

California Closets
    calclosets.com
    888-336-9709
    Custom closets

Carlyle Sofa
    carlylesofa.com
    Armless sofa bed

Charles Rogers
    charlesrogers.com
    Trundle beds

Clos-ette (Holistic Organizational
Design)
    clos-ette.com
    977-803-9797
    Custom closets

Closet World
    closetworld.com
    800-434-6018
    Storage products, including
    for the garage and the
    basement

Closets By Design
    ClosetsByDesign.com
    800-293-3744
    Custom closets

The Company Store
    thecompanystore.com
    800-285-3696
    Three-in-one table

The Container Store
    containerstore.com
    888-CONTAIN
    Organizing products, spice
    racks, Elfa shelving and
    drawer systems

Crate and Barrel
    CrateandBarrel.com
    800-323-5461
    Ashton Sofa, Bayside
    Sofa, Taka Trunk, rattan
    storage ottomans,
    spice racks, Somerset
    Kitchen Island

Curran FLOOR
> curranfloor.com
> 800-555-6653
> Woven vinyl floor
> covering

Design Within Reach
> dwr.com
> 800-944-2233
> Cubits shelving system,
> Sapien Bookcase, Nexus
> Storage Cube, retractable
> "wall," "sliding" sofa,
> counter stools

Dom New York
> 212-253-5969
> Ceiling-mounted range hoods

Door to Door Moving and
Storage
> doortodoor.com
> Moving services:
> 888-505-3667
> Self storage: 888-410-3667
> Moving services and off-site
> storage

The Door Store
> doorstorefurniture.com
> 877-DOOR STORE
> Storage cubes

dVider
> dvider.com
> 212-966-3366
> Room dividers

EasyClosets.com
> Custom closets

Expo
> expo.com
> 800-553-3199

FlatRate Moving
> flatrate.com
> 800-486-FLAT
> Moving services and off-site
> storage

FLOR
> florcatalog.com
> 866-281-FLOR
> Carpet and sisal tiles

FunStuffForDogs.com
> 972-712-2812
> Pet Murphy bed

Gaiam
> gaiam.com
> 877-989-6321
> Organic, mold-resistant
> plasters and pigments

Granite Transformations
> granitetransformations.com
> 866-685-5300
> "Slipcovers" for countertops, backsplashes, and floors

Home Decorator's Collection
> HomeDecorators.com
> 800-245-2217
> Leather furniture with storage options, pedestals

Home Depot
> HomeDepot.com
> Closet organizing and storage products, lighting basics, wooden medicine cabinet frames

HomeFocus
> HomeFocusCatalog.com
> 800-221-6771
> Indoor and outdoor organizing and storage products

Horchow
> horchow.com
> 800-456-7000
> Wooden trays

Improvements
> ImprovementsCatalog.com
> 800-642-2122
> Folding chrome serving cart

Jensen-Lewis
> Jensen-Lewis.com
> Convertible table

KangaRoom Storage
> KangaRoomStorage.com
> 415-543-3615
> Collapsible storage boxes

kitchensource.com
> 800-667-8721
> Pot racks

Kreon
> kreon.com
> uli.petzgold@kreon.us
> Unobtrusive track lighting

Lee's Studio
> leesstudio.com
> 212-581-4400
> Table and floor lamps and lamp shades

Levenger
: Levenger.com
: 800-667-8034
: Office furniture

Lillian Vernon
: lillianvernon.com
: 800-901-9291
: Under-cabinet kitchen
: organizer

Love That Cat
: lovethatcat.com
: Wooden litter boxes

Lowe's
: lowes.com
: 800-445-6937
: Storage for every room in
: the house, lighting basics,
: wooden medicine cabinet
: frames

MetroKitchen
: metrokitchen.com
: 888-892-9911
: Pot racks

Murphy Bed Company
: murphybedcompany.com
: 800-845-2337
: Murphy beds

Murphy Wall-Beds Hardware, Inc.
: murphybeds.com
: 800-667-6336
: Murphy beds

Museum of Modern Art
: momastore.org
: 800-447-6662
: Tools Design aluminum knife
: stand

The Noguchi Museum Store
: akaristore.stores.yahoo.net
: 718-204-7088
: Paper "light sculptures"

Organize.com
: 800-600-9817
: Elfa shelving and drawer
: systems

Organize-It.com
: 617-734-7240
: Bathroom organizing
: products

Organized Living
: organized-living.com
: Organizing products

Oriental Furniture
    OrientalFurniture.com
    800-978-2100
    Screens

Orvis
    orvis.com
    888-235-9763
    Dog beds

PackMate
    PackMate.com
    Closet storage bags

Pier 1 Imports/Loft 21
    Pier1.com
    Convertible desk

Poliform USA
    Poliformusa.com
    888-POLIFORM
    Custom closets

potracks.com
    800-667-8721
    Pot racks

PotRacksGalore
    PotRacksGalore.com
    800-608-9698
    Pot racks

Pottery Barn
    PotteryBarn.com
    800-922-5507
    Table and floor lamps and
    lamp shades, Drew Bedside
    Table, magazine rack,
    Hotel Collection, Olivia
    Wall Shelves

Rakks
    rakks.com
    800-826-6006
    Glass, metal, and wooden
    shelving units

RangeCraft
    rangecraft.com
    201-791-0440
    Pot racks

Resource Furniture
    resourcefurniture.com
    212-753-2039
    Wall-mounted bunk beds

Restoration Hardware
    restorationhardware.com
    800-762-1005
    Carlton Storage Bench, table
    and floor lamps and lamp
    shades, Memo Screen,

storage piece and small
cabinets for the kitchen

Rowe Furniture
rowefurniture.com
800-334-7693
Mini Mod Collection sofas

Sears
Searshomecenter.com
Storage products

Service Caster Corporation
servicecaster.com
800-215-8220
Casters and wheels

The Sharper Image
sharperimage.com
800-344-5555
Library lamp with dimmer,
collapsible elliptical strider

Sirius
siriushoods.com
866-528-4987
Ceiling-mounted range
hoods

Solutions
Solutions.com
800-342-9988
Shower curtain rod with
towel bar

Stacks and Stacks
stacksandstacks.com
800-761-5222
Closet organizing products,
spice racks, back-of-door
combination hamper, towel
rack, and shelf

Target
target.com
800-591-3869
Esprit convertible coffee
table

Touch of Class
touchofclasscatalog.com
800-457-7456
Amelia magazine storage
table

Urban Archaeology
urbanarchaeology.com
Pot racks

West Elm

westelm.com

866-WESTELM

Storage bench, curtains

Williams-Sonoma

williams-sonoma.com

877-812-6235

Pot racks

Williams-Sonoma Home

wshome.com

800-922-4188

Table and floor lamps and
lamp shades, wooden trays,
counter stools

Index

For more information about Use What You Have® Decorator Training and Certification Programs, consultations, seminars, and the Interior Refiners Network,® or to share your before-and-after stories and photos, please visit the Use What You Have® Web site at www.redecorate.com and the Interior Refiners Network® Web site at www.InteriorRefiners.com, or call (800) WE-USE-IT.